READING PLACES, READING PEOPLE

S t u a r t
H y l t o n

 BERKSHIRE BOOKS

First published in 1992 by Berkshire Books

British Library Cataloguing in Publication Data

Hylton, Stuart
Reading Places, Reading People
Illustrated History of the Town
I. Title
942.293

ISBN 0–7509–0060–1

BERKSHIRE BOOKS

Official Imprint of Berkshire County Council
Managed by
Alan Sutton Publishing Ltd
Phoenix Mill · Far Thrupp · Stroud
Gloucestershire

For Sheila, Michael and Philip

Typeset in 11/12 Melior
Typesetting and origination by
Alan Sutton Publishing Ltd
Printed in Great Britain by
The Bath Press, Avon.

Contents

Acknowledgements

I have many people to thank for their help in producing this book. First are the many historians of Reading who have gone before me. Their scholarship and industry have made my task immeasurably easier. I have listed my sources at the back of the book and I hope that readers will be encouraged to learn more about the history of Reading from them. Most of them can be found in the local history section of Reading Central Library.

Berkshire Library Service allowed me to use their collection of photographs and maps. Nick Bond of Berkshire Books, part of Berkshire County Council's Libraries and Information Service, helped me to arrange publication of the book. Particular thanks are due to Margaret Smith for her help with the illustrations and the text.

John Rhodes and his colleagues at Reading Museum have been of great assistance to me. A number of the illustrations in the book are drawn from their collections. Particular thanks go to Godfrey Omer-Parsons and to Sue Read at Blake's Lock Museum.

The Institute of Agricultural History and Museum of English Rural Life at the University of Reading allowed me access to their collection of Victorian photographs. Thanks to Barbara Holden for helping me to find my way around the collection.

Reading Borough Council allowed me to use examples from their collection of old maps to illustrate the book.

Suttons Seeds allowed me to use the photographs of their Market Place premises.

The Trustees of the Science Museum allowed me to reproduce the early photographs of Reading by Fox Talbot from their collection.

Friends and colleagues, too numerous to mention, helped me with reading the manuscript, suggestions on form, content and presentation, and in tracking down sources of information.

If, despite all the efforts of all the above, errors or other shortcomings remain in the book, the responsibility for them is entirely my own.

Last, but by no means least, grateful thanks are due to my wife and sons for putting up with a distracted husband and father during the preparation of this book.

Preface

Though so large portion of the town is of recent growth, and though . . . it has a comparatively modern appearance, Reading is very ancient, and has always been of some importance.
                                        Reading Yearbook, 1880

This is an age which is too ready to wipe out the past and forget those who built up what we now enjoy.
                    The Streets and Street Lore of Reading, 1926

We are not the first generation to feel that Reading is changing with dramatic speed. For the past two hundred years, the canals, the railways and the motorways have in turn brought new industries, new horizons and new pressures for growth to the town.

But even before the coming of the canals, Reading had a thousand years of often turbulent history. The inhabitants of Reading in the ninth century had more reason than most to complain about the pace of change. In the year AD 871, invading Danes sacked and destroyed the settlement.

Despite all the change, there is still much evidence of the town's history for us to see. There are over eight hundred historic buildings in Reading. The pattern of the main streets is recognizably the same as four centuries ago. Even many of the street names tell part of the story of the town.

This book uses the historic buildings and streets of Reading today to tell that story. I hope it will encourage the reader to look afresh at the history that is all around them.

Of course, it is impossible to give a full account of a thousand years of history in these few pages. However, many excellent books have been written about Reading. The town's museums are also rich in local history. I hope readers will be encouraged to find out more.

The Birth of Reading – St Mary's Butts

In the oldest surviving map of the town, dating from 1611 (see page 118), St Mary's Butts is referred to as Olde Strete. Much of the earliest history of the town centred around this area, close to the water supplies of the Holy Brook and the Kennet.

The focal point of the area is St Mary's church, which has a history of over a thousand years of continuous worship. It is known as a minster church, suggesting that it was an important religious centre, serving a wide area, before the Norman Conquest.

The first place of worship on the site was the result of a cruel murder. Queen Elfrida was the mother of Ethelred the Unready and stepmother of Edward, King of the West Saxons. She coveted the throne for her natural son. While the fifteen-year-old King Edward was her guest at Corfe Castle in AD 978, she had him stabbed in the back. He was known thereafter as Edward the Martyr.

A nunnery was said to have been built on the site of St Mary's by Elfrida, in atonement of her sins. No trace has ever been found of the building, which may have been destroyed by Danes when they raided the town in 1006.

Only a doorway in the north wall now survives from the Norman church. The south arcade dates from around 1200, but most of the church, including the tower, was rebuilt in about 1551. The tower, which replaced an earlier steeple, also had a military purpose. Many soldiers could be concealed within it and it provided a valuable look-out post at a time when most of Reading was no more than two storeys. Much of the stone and timber for the 1551 rebuilding came from the demolition of Reading Abbey. Further additions to the church were made in the nineteenth century, when the chancel and north aisle were added.

Edward IV decreed that every Englishman should have a bow

1

of his own height and that every town should have a 'butts' for archery practice every feast day. The name Butts came from the targets or marks used for archery practice, which took place in the street. Hampshire and Berkshire longbowmen, fifty of whom were drawn from Reading, were among the cream of the troops at Agincourt. The laws about maintaining a butts survived well into the era of firearms. In 1602, the town was fined for not maintaining a butts. They finally bought a dispensation to avoid having to keep this outdated practice going in 1631. It cost them £3.

Apart from the church, the area contains buildings covering four hundred years, from examples of timber-framed Elizabethan construction to that 1960s miracle of concrete ugliness, the Broad Street Mall. The Horn public house is a sixteenth-century timber-framed building beneath the later alterations. The original door, on the corner of St Mary's Butts and Castle Street, has been replaced by a window. Across the road, the Allied Arms also dates from the sixteenth century, once again behind a later facade. If you look down the side passage you can see the overhanging jettied upper storey, typical of a building of that period.

St Mary's House, in the churchyard, dates from the first half of the eighteenth century. It was once used as a brewery and was bought by the church in 1919. Although altered on the outside, much of the eighteenth-century interior survives.

Within the churchyard there is a jubilee cross, erected in 1877. It commemorates the nineteenth-century restoration of the church by public subscription and also the generosity of Isaac Harrinson. Harrinson was a surgeon who lived in Castle Street. It was at his instigation and largely at his expense that the festering slums in the middle of St Mary's Butts were demolished around this time.

Among those interred in the north-west corner of the churchyard are said to be criminals executed at Gallows Tree Common in Earley. One nineteenth-century eye-witness recalls seeing a skeleton being exhumed, with chains still attached to his legs and wrists.

As the 1611 map shows, the churchyard was not always open as it is now. The buildings along the Gun Street frontage were demolished around 1816 and the churchyard extended. Around this time, the level of Gun Street was raised considerably. This can be seen from the Old Shades Inn – most recently used as a wine bar on Gun Street near the back of Heelas – which is well below current street level. Until around 1850, the Shades had a lock-up

St Mary's church and the cottages fronting on to the churchyard, seen from Bridge Street in 1886.

at the rear for any prisoners arrested by the nightwatchmen. It may not have been heavily used, since these early custodians of the law were not noted for their courage in tackling criminals.

The almshouses along the St Mary's Butts frontage lasted until 1886, when they were acquired by the corporation for road widening. The history of the almshouses in St Mary's Butts dates back to 1476.

St Mary's Butts has seen its share of the historic events in the life of the town. One such was a giant street party, organized by the corporation in 1814 to celebrate what was thought to be the end of the Napoleonic Wars. The three parishes raised £410 4s. 3d. towards the cost and seven thousand needy people were invited. Eighty tables, laden with beef, veal pies, hot plum puddings and nineteen gallons of beer per table, stretched the length of St Mary's Butts and out as far as London Street and Friar Street. The feast was followed by games in the Forbury Gardens and carousing continued until 6 a.m. the next morning. The local press complained about the extravagance of the corporation. In fact, many of those attending the feast all too rarely saw a square meal. Both nationally and locally, the economy had been crippled by the long war. Poverty, disease and hunger were rife in the town at this time.

The west side of St Mary's Butts in 1880. The Swan Inn on the left of the picture stands on the corner of Hosier Street, where the market is now held.

4

The north end of St Mary's Butts in 1932. The narrow gap is being widened to help traffic movement and Holmes's furniture store has just been demolished.

A culinary event of a more dubious kind occurred in St Mary's Butts during the Second World War. A queue of housewives at Baylis's grocery shop on the Broad Street corner were waiting for a rumoured consignment of tinned salmon. Instead they were offered the first consignment of snoek, a curious and unappetizing relative of the pike that was imported to overcome wartime food shortages. It was well received in Reading, leading the Ministry of Food to import it by the boatload. Then, as now, Reading was held to be a good barometer of national public opinion. On this occasion, unfortunately, snoek was not at all well received in the rest of the country!

St Mary's Butts also has an unexpected link with the history of aviation. From 1877 until after the Second World War, a cycle manufacturer called Warwicks operated from premises in the street. Their products were exported to America, where one of their outlets was run by a pair of young brothers in Dayton, Ohio. The proceeds of their sales were used to help fund their experiments in aeronautics. Their names were Wilbur and Orville Wright.

Reading Abbey

For over four hundred years Reading Abbey dominated the life of the town and made it one of the most important religious and political centres in the country. The few parts of the Abbey that survive today give some idea of its immense scale. By the time of its dissolution, it covered an area of 30 acres, bounded today by Forbury Road, Kings Road, Blagrave Street and the railway. The outer walls stretched for half a mile.

Within those walls was a whole community – a church the size of Westminster Abbey or Durham Cathedral, a hospital, a library, a refectory, accommodation for the poor, a leper colony, a mill, gardens and an abbot's house so grand it needed forty servants to run it. Construction of the Abbey started in 1121 and took almost two hundred years, until the completion of the Lady Chapel in 1314.

The centrepiece of the Abbey, the Great Church, was dedicated by Thomas à Becket on 19 April 1164, in the presence of Henry II. Just six years later, Thomas was to die at Canterbury, at the hands of some of Henry's knights.

The Abbey was founded by Henry I, youngest son of William the Conqueror. It was said that he did so out of grief at the loss of his son off the coast of France. What is certain is that Henry endowed the Abbey generously. Among the gifts were his estates in Reading and the lands to the north-west of Reading, once given to Battle Abbey by William the Conqueror. By the fourteenth century, it was one of the ten richest Benedictine monasteries in England. Parliament was held there on various occasions between the twelfth and fifteenth centuries.

Henry I died in France in December 1135. His body was sewn into a bull's hide and brought back by barge to Reading Abbey for burial amid great ceremony. Some stories even said that he was buried in a solid silver coffin. His alleged 'remains' have been exhumed at regular intervals since, by people digging in the ruins of the Abbey. Folklore also has it that among the holy relics housed in the Abbey was the mummified hand of St James the Apostle.

Even greater ceremony was seen in 1359, when John of Gaunt, son of Edward III, was married to Blanche of Lancaster in Reading. The wedding ceremony alone lasted seven hours and the celebrations that followed went on for twelve weeks. Blanche was described as one of the beauties of her time. Tragically, she was only to survive for ten years after the wedding, before dying of the plague.

In 1520, Hugh Cook Faringdon became Abbot of Reading. He could little have known then that he would be the last abbot, and that the position was to cost him his life. Although he was on friendly terms with Henry VIII, entertaining him at the Abbey, he was not able to accept the idea of Henry as the spiritual head of the Church.

Eventually, in September 1539, Faringdon was arrested and sent to the Tower of London. In the same month the Abbey was formally dissolved. He was brought back to Reading 'to be tried and executed' (the result of the trial was never in doubt) for high treason. He was sentenced to death by hanging, drawing and quartering.

On 14 November, Hugh Faringdon was drawn through the streets of Reading on a hurdle. The route he took on the way to his martyrdom was via New Strete (Friar Street), Gutter Lane (Cross Street), Brode Street (Broad Street), Chayne Lane (Chain Street), Old Strete (St Mary's Butts), Seaven Bridges (Bridge Street), St Giles Strete (Southampton Street), Sievier Strete (Silver Street), London Strete, Schomakers Row (Market Place), and so to the Forbury, where the gibbet stood on the site now occupied by St James RC church. He was hanged and mercifully was dead by the time they removed him from the gibbet, sparing him the further torment of disembowelling and dismemberment. Faringdon was made a saint by Pope Leo XIII in 1895.

The Abbey now became an occasional residence of the king. Part of the Hospitium was used to house the royal horses. The Queen's Stables are shown on the earliest map of Reading (see p. 118).

It was in the reign of Edward VI that the systematic destruction of the Abbey began. The Duke of Somerset, his uncle and the lord protector of the realm, acquired the Abbey. He immediately began to strip it of building materials. Many of them were taken by barge to London. Some found their way to Windsor to repair Windsor Castle. Others were used locally. The rebuilding of St Mary's church used timber and stone from the Abbey. The roof

Two modern views of what Reading Abbey might have looked like in 1539, shortly before its dissolution. They were drawn by R.W. Ford. One is from the south-east, in the area of Orts Road. The other is from the north-west, near the site of what is now Reading station.

Not just one of the earliest surviving photographs of Reading, but a picture taken within a few years of the advent of photography by one of its pioneers, W.H. Fox Talbot. This is the Abbey Gateway in 1845, before its collapse and restoration. Note the open view across the fields towards Caversham. (Science Museum 551/69)

was sold off for £6 10s. 8d., the images and stones from the high altar for £2 6s. 8d. Everything movable was sold.

During the Civil War, the Royalists blew up the nave of the church to provide materials for their fortifications. The Parliamentarian bombardment during the siege of Reading added to the destruction. By the nineteenth century all the good stone work was gone. Only the flint inner walls of the Chapter House still stand to convey some of the scale and grandeur of the old Abbey. The council acquired the ruins in the nineteenth century and have since carried out works to stabilize them.

Other parts of the Abbey also survive. The inner gateway was, for a number of years, used as a classroom by Abbey School. Its most famous pupil was nine-year-old Jane Austen, who joined the school with her sister in 1785. In 1861, the gateway virtually collapsed. Its restoration was supervised by the eminent Victorian architect Giles Gilbert Scott, whose other works included St Pancras station and the restoration of over half the nation's cathedrals.

The Abbey Hospitium was originally built in the year 1196, to provide hospitality to visitors to the Abbey. It was partly rebuilt in 1438, an early example of brick construction in the town. Over the years it was used as a schoolroom, guildhall and stables. During the Civil War it served as a gunpowder store and a barracks. The refectory was demolished in 1786, in order to develop the small town hall (now the Victoria Hall). The remaining dormitory was 'restored' in the nineteenth century by the architect Slingsby Stallwood. It was then used around the turn of the century by Reading University College. Today it forms part of the office development at the rear of the Town Hall. You can see it from the churchyard or from Valpy Street.

The other surviving relic is an archway from the Abbey Mill, which straddles the Holy Brook, just west of Abbey Street.

These are the last remaining remnants of one of the great religious communities of medieval Britain. How different Reading's history might have been, had it not been for the process of destruction that started with the dissolution of the Abbey in 1539.

The Grey Friars of Friar Street

In October 1224, a group of nine penniless Franciscan monks from Italy landed in Dover. They were lodged at Canterbury, where they began recruiting others to their order. Within ten years, their numbers had grown to nearly a thousand.

It was in 1234 that a group of monks arrived in Reading. They brought with them a letter from Pope Gregory IX, requiring the Abbot of Reading to give them a plot of land on which to build a friary. The Abbot was none too pleased to see a rival monastic order set up in the town, but he could not ignore the Pope's letter. Instead, he gave them the swampiest bit of land he could lay his hands on. It was on the south bank of the Thames near Caversham Bridge.

The Franciscans tried to make a living on this marshy site, but they often found themselves completely cut off from the town by mud and water. In 1285 they sought the help of the Archbishop of Canterbury, himself a Franciscan, and within three years they were given the site on which Greyfriars church now stands, at the end of Friar Street. There they built a large church, completed in 1311. The main elements of it survive to this day as the most complete example of Franciscan architecture in Britain.

The friars continued their work until the church was surrendered to the Crown during the dissolution of the monasteries in 1538. A Doctor John London was sent by Thomas Cromwell to oversee its closure. Most of the land and buildings were sold to a groom of the king's chamber called Robert Stanshawe. Thomas Vachell, the town's member of parliament, and also in the service of Thomas Cromwell, became custodian of the Abbey plate and other valuables. It was he who helped secure the use of the Greyfriars church as a guildhall in 1543.

Dr London not only closed down the Grey Friars and disposed of their valuables, he also defaced the internal decoration of the church and its stained glass windows. What he started, the poor people of Reading finished. The minute the friars had left, they

Greyfriar's church in a ruinous state, before its restoration of 1863.

began looting the friary of anything that was valuable and portable. So began three centuries of decay for the building.

After the guildhall, from about 1570 on, it was used as a hospital and workhouse and then as the town bridewell or gaol. Descriptions of the building at the start of the nineteenth century paint a sorry picture. The roof had been removed at around the turn of the century, to stop it from collapsing. Inside the roofless shell, the outer aisles were roughly divided up into primitive cells of a most dehumanizing kind. Only with the construction of the new county gaol at the Forbury in 1844 did the bridewell fall into disuse.

In 1863, the roofless ruins were restored at a cost of £12,000 as a church by W. H. Woodman. He was the borough surveyor at that time. Part of the eastern end of the church had been totally destroyed and was not included in the scheme. However, some of the medieval floor tiles were saved, as were the arcade and the large west window, with its delicate tracery. The names of some of the prisoners scratched into the pillars can still be seen today, reminding us of its days as a bridewell.

Many of the older buildings along Friar Street itself have been lost, but some remain. The Mitre Inn, on the corner of Friar Street and West Street, dates from at least 1800 and is probably older.

The north side of Friar Street in about 1880. Visible on the left are the entrance to the Hospital for Sick and Lame Horses and the Blagrave buildings.

Although it is no longer known as the Mitre, its original name can still be seen in raised lettering on the wall. Numbers 11, 13 and 15 Friar Street are all eighteenth-century buildings. Outside the Town Hall, the statue of Queen Victoria dates from 1857 and is the work of George Blackall Simonds, a member of the local brewing family. His other work includes the lion in the Forbury Gardens and a statue of a falconer in New York's Central Park. The story goes that Queen Victoria faces the station because she did not like the town and could not wait to leave it!

The Elizabethans and the Oracle

By the end of Queen Elizabeth I's reign, Reading was as we see it on the John Speed map of 1611. It was roughly triangular, bounded in the north by the Abbey and Greyfriars church and in the south by what is now Whitley Street.

Queen Elizabeth was a regular visitor to Reading, sometimes staying in part of the Abbey that had not yet been dismantled for its building materials. She attended services in St Laurence's church and in 1575 had her own special pew provided there, screened off from the rest of the congregation. She also gave an important new charter to the town in 1560, greatly extending its powers of self-government.

John Kendrick was a Reading-born man who made a fortune as a clothing manufacturer in London. When he died in 1624, he left £7,500 to Reading Corporation to provide a workhouse where the poor of Reading might be employed in the clothing industry. It was this inheritance that was eventually to help found Kendrick School.

The site chosen for the workhouse, in Minster Street, was owned by John Kendrick's brother, William. He sold it to the council in 1625 for £2,000. It covered an area of about two acres and the Holy Brook ran through the middle of it. In 1627 work began to construct a series of workshops around a central courtyard. Local brickmaker William Brockman was contracted to supply 200,000 serviceable bricks and 20,000 large and serviceable tiles at 12s. 6d. per thousand. Construction was completed in the middle of 1628.

The unusual name 'Oracle' means ' a person of great wisdom' or 'a response to an appeal to a god'. It is difficult to see why such a name should be given to a workhouse and a variety of explanations have been suggested. One is that it is a corruption of the words 'work hall'. Another suggestion is that it is named after *oricello*, an Italian dye used in the clothing industry. Yet another possibility is that it comes from the word *oriolum*, meaning porch or entrance. Contemporary

Queen Elizabeth I, who provided Reading with an important charter.

John Kendrick (1574–1624), benefactor of the Oracle.

pictures show the Oracle having an imposing entrance (see opposite).

Kendrick's inheritance was badly mismanaged by the corporation. A number of Kendrick's own wealthy relatives used it to subsidize their own businesses, putting their rivals out of business and creating more poverty, rather than less, in the town. In 1639, word of this reached William Laud, Archbishop of Canterbury. He was the son of a Reading clothier, born in Broad Street. Laud made the corporation use the money to buy land between Redlands Road and Silver Street, and between London Road and Christchurch Road. The money from the rents was to be used for charitable works.

This the council did, but the Oracle itself fell into disuse. During the Civil War it was used as a barracks. Afterwards, with the cloth-making industry in Reading by then defunct, it was used as an ordinary workhouse. Later still, by now crumbling from lack of maintenance, it was turned into warehouses and workshops. By the nineteenth century it had become a home for petty criminals.

In 1849 the governors of Christ's Hospital in London came to Reading. Kendrick had provided in his will that, if his inheritance were misused, it could be claimed by the Hospital. This

The Oracle Gateway in 1845, shortly before its demolition. This is one of several photographs of it taken by W.H. Fox Talbot. (Science Museum 543/69)

they were able to do in the courts. In 1850, the Oracle was finally demolished. One small part of the bequest did not pass to the Hospital, due to a clause in Kendrick's will. This was used to fund the establishment of the Kendrick Schools. The boys' school was absorbed into Reading School in the First World War, but the girls' school remains in London Road, near to Kendrick Road, to this day.

The council bought the Oracle site back from Christ's Hospital in 1852. The Hospital had proposed to allow a large number of slum properties to be built on the site, which would have frustrated the council's efforts to improve the area. Today, the original Oracle site, along with other land in the area, is earmarked for a major shopping, office and leisure development. The development will bear the name of the Oracle, providing us with a continuing reminder of one of Reading's most generous benefactors.

The Siege of Reading and the Battle of Caversham Bridge

The Civil War divided and impoverished Reading. The town was occupied by one side or the other throughout the war, with both sides making heavy demands of money and provisions for their troops. There were also divided loyalties among the townspeople. Among local landowning families, the Knollys were for Parliament, the Blounts of Mapledurham and the Englefields of Whiteknights for the king. Some local families, such as the Vachells and the Blagraves, were divided among themselves.

It was in April 1643 that Reading became the first town in England to be besieged. Three thousand Royalist troops, under Sir Arthur Aston, were occupying the town when the Earl of Essex, with 16,000 Parliamentary infantry and 3,000 cavalry, arrived at Caversham Heights. On 15 April they started shelling the town, which had been heavily fortified.

After a heavy bombardment, the Parliamentary troops closed in on the town. St Giles' church was badly damaged and the Royalist commander had been badly injured by a falling roof tile. Colonel Richard Fielding, who took over as commander, sent word to the king that they could not hold out much longer.

The Royalists were desperately short of ammunition. A young ensign named Rupert Flower was sent through the enemy lines to get word to the Royalist ammunition store at Henley. This he did, swimming the Thames and swinging through the trees of Caversham Park above the tents of the Parliamentary reserve troops. He was told to return to Reading, with news of their plan to send supplies up the river by barge at night. On the way back he was captured and tortured into revealing the plan. The barge was captured and the Royalists were virtually out of powder by the time help finally arrived.

Relief forces were on their way from Oxford, but they were met by a group of Parliamentary cavalry at Dorchester. After a fierce battle, the Royalists were routed. By 25 April Fielding decided

St Giles, in Southampton Street, damaged in the Civil War. The photograph pre-dates its restoration in 1871–3.

Caversham church in about 1794. The wooden tower replaced the earlier structure, damaged during the Battle for Caversham Bridge. It was, in turn, replaced during the restoration of the church in 1878/9.

that their position was hopeless. He raised the white flag and began negotiating terms of surrender with the Parliamentarians. At this moment, a strong Royalist force arrived on Caversham Heights. It was led by Prince Rupert, and Charles I himself was with them. The Battle of Caversham Bridge began.

A large, mud-walled barn stood between the Royalists and the bridge. It could only be approached across an open field and a violent hailstorm was blowing into the faces of the Royalist troops. As they crossed the field, the Royalists were cut down by gunfire 'like ripe fruit in a strong wind'. Local people afterwards talked of the day that 'Balmayers field ran blood'. This field was to give its name to Balmore House, built there in 1834.

The Royalists were defeated and retreated up a track, which is now the old Peppard Road. Some of the fiercest fighting is said to have taken place on the fields of Emmer Green, close to the Royalist stronghold of Caversham Park.

On 27 April 1643, the Royalist garrison surrendered. Under the terms of the surrender, they were allowed to march out of the town and rejoin the king at Oxford, taking with them fifty carts carrying their sick and wounded, and such weaponry as they had left.

The Parliamentary troops were then billeted upon the town. Despite undertakings given by the Earl of Essex, some of the houses of leading Royalists were looted and there were some ugly scenes of violence. Several weeks of heavy drinking and widespread disorder followed, until Essex marched his troops away in July.

Reading changed hands several times during the course of the Civil War. The war had a ruinous effect upon the town and the surrounding countryside. The area was stripped of food and horses; soldiers stole from the people and threatened them; the council and many of the leading citizens of the town were reduced to poverty by the demands of the warring parties on them. In 1644 the mayor of Reading, William Brackstone, was kidnapped by the Royalists to help them extort money from the council. Added to all this, the town had a serious visitation of the plague in 1646, in which hundreds died.

The final act of the war came in January 1649, when the death warrant of King Charles I was signed. One of the fifty-nine members of parliament to put their names to it was the member for Reading, Daniel Blagrave. On his way to his eventual execution, Charles I stayed at Caversham Park, where his children were allowed to visit him.

An early view of the mound in Forbury Gardens, all that remains of the Civil War fortifications.

For the most part, the Civil War brought only destruction to the town. But one memento of those times stands in Reading today. The large mound in the Forbury Gardens is all that remains of the extensive fortifications built at the time of the Civil War.

Going Up, Coming Down

Change has been a fact of life in Reading for many years. The photographs in this section show some examples.

Tramlines being laid at Cemetery Junction in 1901.

The wreckage of Reading Abbey gateway, which virtually collapsed in 1861.

The demolition of 45–50 St Mary's Butts in 1886.

The demolition of the old Caversham Bridge in 1869.

Worship and Persecution – Reading's Churches

ST LAURENCE'S

A number of Reading's churches can lay claim to a history almost as long as that of Reading Abbey. In the case of St Laurence's church in Friar Street, it originally was part of the Abbey. The outer gate of the Abbey adjoined the south wall of the church.

The church was founded here in about 1121, although there are suggestions that an older church on the site of the Abbey itself may have been relocated to this spot. Legend has it that St Laurence's was built by an apprentice of the builder of St Mary's church. When he saw how superior the work of his apprentice was, the builder of St Mary's is said to have thrown himself from the tower of his own church.

The oldest part of the church is a small round-headed window high in the south wall, which dates from about 1121. The church was enlarged in 1196, probably at the same time as St John's Hospitium was being built nearby. The north aisle and St John's chapel, and the arcade between the chapel and the chancel, all date from about 1210. Its windows and the tower are rather later, dating from about the middle of the fifteenth century.

Until the middle of the nineteenth century, a covered arcade ran along the south side of the church. It was called Blagrave's Piazza, after the mathematician John Blagrave who provided the money to have it built. It was completed in 1619. One of the uses of the Piazza was to store the town's stocks, pillory and tumbril, which were taken out into nearby Market Place when required. It was also the scene of much vice and depravity, according to one nineteenth-century observer, who described the Piazza as 'a most clumsy and ill-formed arcade . . . erected in defiance of every rule of architecture'. Contemporary pictures show this judgement to be rather unfair (see page 39).

St Mary's church. This is another Fox-Talbot photograph from 1845, prior to the restoration of the church. Note the lack of trees in the churchyard. (Science Museum 533/69)

The church was excessively restored at a cost of £12,000 in 1869. Part of the original west window, which was removed at this time, now stands as a monument in the churchyard. More recently, the pinnacles on top of the church tower had to be removed, following bomb damage in 1943.

Much of the life of the town has centred around St Laurence's. In the fifteenth century, May Day celebrations were held outside its west door, with a maypole and performances of plays about Robin Hood. During the reign of Mary Tudor, Julius Palmer, the master of Reading School, was exhibited in a cage above the gate of St Laurence's churchyard, before his eventual trial and martyrdom.

The church has a long history of links with royalty. Queen Elizabeth I worshipped there and it also received endowments from Henry II, Henry VII and James I. During the Civil War it was used as a barracks, and the churchwardens' records show they had to spend 3s. 4d. to repair damage to the seats by the soldiers and 1s. on frankincense 'to sweeten the church'. For many years, prisoners hanged at Reading gaol were buried in the east corner of the churchyard.

ST GILES'

St Giles' church in Southampton Street has existed since at least 1191 when it was granted to Reading Abbey. Like St Laurence's, it was the victim of a Victorian 'restoration' by J.P. St Aubyn, which removed many of its original features.

St Giles was the patron saint of blacksmiths, cripples and beggars, and churches to him were often built on the edge of towns. It was originally built because the River Kennet, just to the north, used to flood and turn itself into a mudflat in winter. Worshippers living to the south were then cut off from St Mary's.

One of the vicars of St Giles', John Eynon, was martyred alongside Hugh Faringdon in 1539. During the Civil War, it is said that the Royalists had a gun mounted on the tower of St Giles'. This attracted the attention of the enemy artillery and resulted in the destruction of the tower. The present tower is built of conglomerate, a local building stone consisting of gravel pebbles set in a kind of natural concrete.

FRIENDS' MEETING HOUSE, CHURCH STREET

Many of the town's churches stand as a reminder of the religious persecution that is part of Reading's history. The present Friends' Meeting House dates from about 1835, but Quakers have a much longer tradition of worship in Reading.

George Fox, the founder of the Quakers, first came to Reading in 1655. He preached to a large crowd in an orchard on the south side of London Road and also at the Market Place. One of the earliest converts was Thomas Curtis, a wool merchant of Silver Street, who let the group use his house for some of their first meetings.

The Quakers were much persecuted in their early years. By the time Fox returned to Reading in 1670, most of his fellow worshippers were in prison, seven of them dying there. Among their main persecutors at this time were George Thorn, who was mayor of Reading and Sir William Armorer, equerry to the king.

The latter appears to have been a particularly vicious character, beating the male worshippers with a staff, pulling their wives' noses and pricking their children with a goad!

Another notable Quaker to come to Reading was William Penn, the founder of Pennsylvania. He preached in Sims Court, just off London Street (behind what was until recently the London Street Bookshop). In Pennsylvania, USA, today there is a Berkshire County, the main town of which is called Reading.

John Bunyan also came to Reading to preach. He entered the town disguised as a carter to avoid detection and held a service at Coley Street.

ST MARY'S, CASTLE STREET

This church was built as the result of a dispute among the congregation of St Giles'. A number of them disapproved of their new vicar, Joseph Eyre, and in 1798 built a church on the site of the old Reading gaol. Its most striking feature, the Corinthian portico in Bath stone, was a later addition. It was added in 1842 by prominent local architects, Henry and Nathaniel Briant. Other important buildings in Reading for which they were responsible are the Royal Berkshire Hospital and the former Simonds Bank building in King Street.

The church used to have a most unusual bell tower, known locally as 'the pepper box', which looked rather like an old-fashioned telephone kiosk. It became unsafe in the 1950s and had to be removed.

ST JAMES' ROMAN CATHOLIC CHURCH, FORBURY ROAD

The Quakers were not the only ones to be subjected to religious persecution. Sir Francis Knollys was only one of a number of enthusiastic Catholic priest-hunters, and shared Archbishop Laud's taste for nailing his opponents to the pillory by their ears. It is only relatively recently that Catholics were able to build their own permanent places of worship in Reading.

St James' church is built on the site next to Reading gaol, where the public executions used to be held. It is largely built of stone from Reading Abbey. The architect was the son of a refugee from the French Revolution, Augustus Welby Pugin. He is better

A drawing of St Mary's in Castle Street, dating from between the wars.

known as the architect of parts of the Houses of Parliament, including the tower of Big Ben. The church dates from 1840 and is thought to be the only one he built in the Norman style. The font is an intricately carved stone found in the ruins of Reading Abbey. The church was extended in the twentieth century. The site for the church and part of its cost of construction were met by James Wheble, who lived at Bulmershe Court and was a leading member of the local Catholic community.

Reading's Historic Bridges

CAVERSHAM BRIDGE

Reading and Caversham were both established settlements by the time of the Domesday survey. For as long as the two settlements have existed, people have been crossing the river Thames which lay between them.

The very earliest crossings may have been by means of a ford. It is thought that one existed near the site of Caversham Mill, linking the site of Reading Abbey with the Manor of Caversham. No doubt it would have been impassable for parts of the year.

A ferry existed from the early days of Reading's history. In the year 1231, Henry III gave an order to the keeper of Windsor Forest 'to deliver to Andrew, Sergeant of Caversham, one good oak to make a boat for ferrying poor people over the water of Caversham'. Ferries continued to operate into the twentieth century, and one of the Victorian ferrymen was to give his name to a Reading landmark.

In the same year that that oak was felled, we find the first reference to Caversham Bridge. The Close Rolls of 1231 refer in particular to a chapel 'on the bridge of Tamisiam, founded partly by the Abbot of Reading and partly by William, Earl Marshall'. It was a timber bridge and very narrow. The chapel combined the role of a shrine, at which travellers might seek spiritual refreshment, and a place for collecting bridge tolls. The bridge being in shared ownership, tolls were collected at both ends, so crossing may have been an expensive business, explaining why the poor people needed a ferry.

In the mid-1300s, the chapel passed with other property in Caversham into the gift of Notley Abbey. In 1366 it was valued at 100s. After the dissolution of the Abbey, Henry VIII sold it to his cofferer, Anthony Brigham. It remained in his family until the 1920s, when the council bought the island on which the chapel had stood to build the present Caversham Bridge.

The chapel was all but gone by then, and a fisherman's cottage had been built on its foundations. The last traces of the chapel, which was dedicated to St Anne, were incorporated in a new shrine in the Roman Catholic church in South View Avenue.

The bridge itself appears to have spent large parts of its life in a ruinous state. In 1480, the people of Reading complained to Edward VI about the Abbot's negligence in maintaining it. During the Civil War, the Reading end of the bridge (which was at that time a drawbridge) was partly dismantled as a defensive measure. When Charles I heard of this, he gave orders that the bridge should be made ready for his troops to cross by 8 a.m. the following morning. In fact, records show that repairs were not completed until two years later, in 1644.

By the early nineteenth century, the bridge was in a ruinous state again. In 1812, a carter named Barefoot fell to his death in the Thames, as a result of most of the parapet of the bridge being missing. Two years later, part of the bridge collapsed entirely. It was repaired by local resident William Blandy, who was repaid by public subscription. One of the reasons for the bridge's ruinous state seems to have been that there was no clear responsibility for its upkeep.

The bridge was largely renewed in 1830. Typically, the Caversham half was in stone, and the Reading half in wood and

The 'half-and-half' Caversham Bridge that survived until 1869.

The iron bridge that spanned the Thames from 1869 to 1926. The remains of the old bridge can be seen beneath the new iron construction.

iron. This arrangement lasted until 1869, when it was replaced by an all-iron bridge. The choice of iron was no doubt influenced by the fact that Caversham Park was then occupied by the Crawshays, the family of ironmasters who had founded the great ironworks at Merthyr Tydfil.

During the construction of this bridge, the ferryman's cottage had to be moved *en masse* by 8ft. This was done using a recently developed American technique. All the furniture is said to have remained inside the three-storey cottage during the move. The entire operation took about three hours and not a single pane of glass was apparently broken in the move. The ferryman was known as 'old man Piper' and Piper's Island, in the middle of the Thames by Caversham Bridge, is named after him.

The new iron bridge was an inelegant structure, looking like an army surplus item. There were widespread complaints about its appearance when it was first built and it soon proved to be too narrow to carry the growing flows of traffic.

By 1911, both sides of the bridge came within Reading Borough. As part of the boundary review that brought Caversham into Reading, it was proposed to replace the old Caversham

High Bridge on Duke Street. A sketch by local artist Alfred Rawlings, dating from 1897.

Bridge. A start on this was delayed by the First World War and work on it only began in 1924. The official opening by the king was further delayed by the General Strike. Finally, on 25 June 1926, the present Caversham Bridge was officially opened, the latest in a seven-hundred-year history of bridges across this part of the Thames.

HIGH BRIDGE, DUKE STREET

The history of bridge building across the Kennet is probably as long as that of Caversham Bridge. The earliest maps of the town show a crossing of the Kennet at Duke Street. For most of the eighteenth century, this was provided by a wooden bridge, erected in 1707. This bridge was the subject of a royal visit in 1738, when the Prince and Princess of Wales came up the Kennet in their royal barge, and were received at the bridge 'with loud acclamations' by the people of Reading.

The present structure, High Bridge, dates from 1787. It was designed by an architect called Robert Brettingham of Hanover Square, London. He also worked on Longleat House and on the original prison at Forbury Road. The bridge cost £3,500 to build.

At the time when it was built, the 109 ft barges that traded along the Kennet had to go through it on a slant. An island in the middle of the river, just upstream of the bridge, made this part of the Kennet especially difficult to navigate.

The bridge is now one of Reading's three scheduled ancient monuments.

READING BRIDGE AND 'THE CLAPPERS'

Reading Bridge is a newcomer by comparison to the others. The recommendation to build it came from the Boundary Commission in 1911. It was completed in 1923 and was tested by assembling a vast number of steam rollers and heavily-laden lorries on it. Quite what would have happened, had the bridge failed the test, does not bear thinking about! The first real traffic to pass over it was rather less of a load – the Caversham and Reading Laundry delivery wagon, pulled by a horse called Charlie.

Before this, the only crossing at this point was by a rickety footbridge across the lock and weir, known as 'the Clappers'. This had been in existence since at least 1603, when it was referred to as 'Le Clopper'. The present structure replaced it after the Second World War. It was from the Clappers that the notorious Victorian murderess, Annie Dyer, threw her infant victims. For years after, local people were said to visit the scene of the crime and carve the sign of the cross in the handrail in memory of the murdered children.

The 1688 Revolution – the Battle of Market Place

The Revolution of 1688, in which the Catholic James II was deposed by William of Orange, was known as the bloodless revolution. This is not strictly correct. A battle, in which up to fifty lives were lost, was fought in the streets of Reading. The people of Reading themselves took part in it.

James had placed the bulk of his force at Hounslow Heath, but had stationed an advance guard of several hundred in Reading. These troops, all Irish Catholics, were hated and feared by the people of Reading. Rumours abounded that they intended to plunder the town and murder its inhabitants.

William landed at Torbay in November 1688 and led his Dutch troops towards London. As soon as the Dutch were close enough to contact, at Hungerford, Reading Corporation managed to get a message to William, seeking help. He sent a force of 250 troops to relieve the town.

The Irish expected the Dutch to come along the Bath Road. They posted cavalry in Castle Street, musketeers in St Mary's churchyard, more troops in Broad Street, with the main body in Market Place. A lookout was posted in the tower of St Mary's church to give early warning of the enemy's arrival.

The townspeople managed to get word of these preparations to the Dutch, who cut across to what is now Oxford Road (then a lane leading to Pangbourne). They caught the Irish completely by surprise. One body of Dutch troops swept down St Mary's Butts and took on the Irish contingent there. The rest overwhelmed the troops in Broad Street. The Irish retreated in confusion along Minster Street, Broad Street, and London Street.

Although the Irish outnumbered the Dutch, the main contingent in Market Place misread the situation. They began to flee, with the people of Reading adding to their confusion with musket fire from the windows of their houses. The Dutch chased them as far as Twyford, killing or wounding fifty-three of the

Market Place from near St Laurence's church, in around 1880.

Irish troops for the loss of about six of their own. Some of the dead are buried in St Giles' churchyard. The church bells were rung in Reading that day, and for over a century afterwards 9 December was celebrated by local people.

Some of the buildings in Market Place today are the same ones from which the people of Reading fired on the departing troops in 1688. The four-storey timber-framed building at numbers 27–8 dates from the early seventeenth century or even before. The shopfront dates from around 1760. The Coopers Arms at numbers 29–31, is also seventeenth century, though it has been altered since. The exposed timbering on the front is false, but the inside contains some re-used fittings from an even older house, possibly dating from Elizabethan times. The door to number 29 is a fine example, dating from about 1600.

Lloyds Bank in Market Place stands on the site of an historic inn, 'The Broad Face'. Samuel Pepys noted it in his diaries and, in 1655, the Society of Friends held some of their earliest meetings on its bowling green with their founder, George Fox. Polling took place there in 1847. Thomas Noon Talfourd, elected as Liberal MP, drank too much punch and ended the celebration in a horizontal position. The inn survived until the 1920s.

St Laurence's church. A photograph dating from before 1868, when the Blagrave Piazza on the south side of the church was demolished.

Some of the old houses in Market Place. A picture dating from 1926.

Some of the newer features of Market Place are also of interest. The obelisk in the middle was designed by Sir John Soane and dates from 1804. It commemorates Edward Simeon, a member of a wealthy family who lived on the Forbury. A former mayor of Reading and one-time governor of the Bank of England, Simeon was also a benefactor of the poor. He organized tea parties for poor children and distributed clothes among them. He left a sum to pay for his monument to be illuminated for all time by the corporation.

An attractive drinking fountain is set into the south wall of St Laurence's church. It was presented to the town in 1860 by Thomas Rogers, clerk to the Local Board of Health and has a water lily motif carved into the stonework. It was restored in 1990. The original inscription on the fountain (now illegible) reads 'The Fear of the Lord is a fountain of life'.

Another notable nineteenth-century addition was the Renaissance-style London and County Bank (now occupied by the National Westminster Bank), which dates from 1875. There is also an interesting example of art nouveau building in High Street, dating from 1904.

On the west side of Market Place is the gateway to the former corn exchange, erected in 1854. The gateway is all that remains of it. The area behind suffered some of the worst effects of the one raid on Reading by German bombers in the Second World War.

A worse fate than bombing almost overtook Market Place in the 1960s. Plans were drawn up to redevelop it comprehensively, and some of the monstrosities were actually built before the idea was shelved. It is to be hoped that these latest additions to this historic part of Reading will only be a short-lived blot on the landscape.

Canals and Coaches

From the earliest days, when the Danes sailed down the Thames on their mission of destruction, the waterways have been an important channel of communication for Reading. Reading's growth as a manufacturing centre was built on the use of the canal to distribute its products.

For a long time, High Bridge was the limit of navigation on the Kennet. The town therefore also became an important distribution centre for goods coming into the area. Wharves were built along the banks of the Kennet. In 1404 the Abbey and the Merchants' Guild agreed rules for the passage of boats along the Kennet. Tolls of 1d. each way and 2d. for 'strangers' were charged for the use of the river.

Although many grand proposals were put forward to link London and Bristol via the Avon and the Thames, the first practical improvement plans for the waterways involved making the Kennet navigable as far as Newbury. Reading people strongly opposed the idea, fearing loss of trade, but in 1715 the Kennet Navigation Act was passed and work began.

In 1720, the opposition of Reading people turned to violence. A mob of about three hundred, including the mayor, Robert Blake, smashed up part of the canal works. Their efforts were in vain, for in 1724 the Kennet Navigation opened to trade. Hostility to the bargemen continued. They were stoned as they passed through the town and one at least received an anonymous death threat. Mill owners along the canal also competed with the barges for the limited supply of water. From the earliest days, water was in short supply in the Kennet – a problem which still exists today.

By the 1740s it was quite clear that the new navigation was in fact making Reading very prosperous. Barges of up to 200 tons traded along it. In 1794, the long-awaited plans for the Kennet and Avon Canal received parliamentary approval, and in 1810 the link between London and Bristol was completed. The first steam barges made their appearance shortly afterwards, in 1813,

Crane Wharf on the Kennet. A sketch from 1897 by Alfred Rawlings.

and three years later the first seagoing boat came up the river as far as High Bridge.

The commercial success of the canal was relatively short lived. In 1840, the railways came to Reading. The canal could not compete and trade fell calamitously. In 1852 it was acquired by the Great Western Railway Company. Not surprisingly, they had little interest in maintaining it and, by the time the railways were nationalized in 1947, it was in very poor condition. Attempts to abandon it entirely in the 1950s met with strong public opposition. After many years of patient restoration, the canal finally reopened to leisure traffic in 1990.

There are many reminders of the days when the canal was an important artery of trade. Bear Wharf, just off Bridge Street, became one of the most important wharves in the town. The Canal Company opened an office, canal house and coal yard there. The wharf was later filled in when trade declined and was used as part of the Simonds Brewery complex.

The huge malthouse in Fobney Street and the building opposite County Lock date back to when Reading was one of the major malting centres of the nation. In the 1880s, Simonds Brewery bought up the towpath between Duke Street and Bridge Street and built on it. The river was forced into a deep, narrow and winding channel called Brewery Gut. Without a towpath, bargees had to get through as best they could using towlines, poles and other devices. The channel was virtually impassable in times of flood, and collisions and sinkings were not uncommon.

Near to the former Huntley and Palmers' factory on King's Road is a small garden, which used to be used by their employees. This was once a wharf where slate and stone for building were unloaded. The slate was brought by schooner from north Wales to Bristol, where it was transferred onto canal barges for the journey to Reading. Huntley and Palmers used the canals for transporting their biscuits until after the Second World War. Not only were they cheaper, but also the smoother form of transport meant that fewer biscuits were broken.

The names along the river also tell part of its history. Blake's Lock is a reminder of the Blake family. Robert Blake was the mayor of Reading who was involved in the riot in 1720 and the family owned land along that stretch of the Kennet. Crane Wharf was formerly called High Bridge Wharf and was owned by William Blandy, an ironmonger and twice mayor of Reading. In 1813 he

Mill Lane, around 1900. A rare view of the industrial Kennet. In the background are the water tower and the mill, both prominent Reading landmarks into the early years of the twentieth century.

installed a crane there, from which the wharf takes its name.

Gunter's Brook, the small stream that joins the Kennet near to the new Queens Road car park, takes its name from Nicholas Gunter. He was a landowner and, again, mayor of Reading at around the time of Queen Elizabeth I.

St Giles' Mill gave its name to Mill Lane, which later became the headquarters of Reading Transport. The last mill on this site was demolished in 1901, ending a tradition of milling there that is thought to have dated back to the Domesday Book. In the early nineteenth century, 20,000 sacks of flour left there each year for London.

COACHES

It was Queen Anne who was largely responsible for the fashion of taking the waters at Bath. In the early part of the eighteenth century crowds of people followed her from London along the

Bath Road. Reading, like all the towns along the road, benefited from the passing trade that the travellers brought.

Coaching inns became some of the most important centres of activity in the town. Old established inns, like the George, the Crown and the Bear, flourished and were extended. New ones grew up to meet the extra demand. In some cases, where the inn stood on a cramped site, expansion caused problems. The Sun, for example, had to build its stables underground. The smells percolated upwards into the guests' bedrooms, making this arrangement less than universally popular!

Competition between the coach operators was fierce. One contemporary writer tells the story of a Dutch auction carried out by two coach operators in the bar of the Turk's Head. Competing for the custom of a traveller, they managed to talk the fare to London down from 10s. to 5s.

The inns also served the local people. At election time, the town experienced an upsurge in drunkenness as parliamentary candidates bought lavish dinners and other hospitality for would-be voters. Political meetings were held there and, in 1814, the Lamb in London Street was indicted at the assizes as 'a house of ill-fame'. French prisoners were billeted in the stables of the Saracen's Head in London Road in 1813. The King's Arms on Castle Hill also played host to around two hundred Frenchmen in 1796, in this case priests exiled from their homeland by the French Revolution. The poet Samuel Taylor Coleridge hid from his creditors by joining the 15th Light Dragoons. They were billeted at the Bear in Bridge Street. Coleridge's unlikely pseudonym, Silas Tomkins Comberpatch, was soon seen through by the authorities and he was returned to his family.

The coming of the railways rapidly killed off the coaching business. By 1841, Reading was linked by rail to both London and Bristol. Within a year or two, the last coach ran between London and Bristol. Despite some attempts to attract the new rail-borne travellers by providing transport to and from the station, the coaching inns fell into a long period of decline.

A number of the inns of the coaching era remain today. The Sun on Castle Street is a seventeenth century timber-framed building on much older foundations. Part of the cellars are alleged to be the remains of the old Reading gaol and there is a Norman arch in the rear yard.

The George, at the junction of King Street and Minster Street, has a history going back as least as far as 1423. In that year

The Sun Inn, Castle Street, one of Reading's ancient coaching inns. The picture dates from around 1880. Behind can be seen St Mary's church with its curious steeple 'the Pepper Box'.

Richard Bedwyn, a former mayor of Reading, willed the reversion of the 'George Syn' to the mayor of the day, to be retained for the use of the guildhall (which then stood nearby). The present building dates mainly from the eighteenth and nineteenth centuries. The King Street frontage is a modern fake of a timber-framed building, but some original timbers survive in it. The interior courtyard area is mostly eighteenth century. A ghost, said to be that of a Civil War cavalier, is rumoured to haunt the inn.

The King's Arms Inn on Castle Street survives, but is now in residential use. It dates from the eighteenth century and stands on three sides of a courtyard. Numbers 158–60 Castle Street are the oldest part of the inn, and date back at least as far as 1734. The third side of the courtyard (154–6 Castle Street) had been added by 1796, when the exiled French priests were billeted there. The group of houses was originally known as 'The Forlorn Hope', after the Civil War outpost set up there by the occupying forces.

Sheep, Sailcloth and Sauce – Some Early Reading Industries

Long before Reading became known for its beer, biscuits and bulbs, it was an important manufacturing town.

WOOLLEN CLOTH

Many of the earliest fortunes that were made in Reading came from the cloth-making industry. We know that a fulling mill (where the woollen cloth was cleaned and thickened by washing) was operating near St Giles' church as early as 1220. A dyeing house was built by the Kennet in 1221 and the cloth-making industry must have been responsible for much of the early pollution of the town's water courses. On market days, the south side of Broad Street was lined with sheep pens, as farmers brought their flocks to market and sold the fleeces to the cloth makers.

The heyday of the town's cloth industry was in the fifteenth and sixteenth centuries. Standards were maintained by the Merchants' Guild, under powers granted to them in a charter by Henry VII in 1487. They inspected each roll of cloth and attached a leaden seal to it if it was up to standard. An official called the alnager had wide-ranging powers to inspect cloth and condemn any that was substandard. He was not a universally popular figure and on one occasion the mayor of Reading had to intervene to stop him being lynched!

The cloth industry was already in decline by the time the Oracle was being built. It was gradually overtaken by more modern manufacturers in the north of England and overseas. Reading's last real link with the cloth and clothing industries was broken by the closure of the raincoat manufacturer in Mill Lane in the 1980s.

Watlington House, in Watlington Street, stands as a reminder of the days when Reading's prosperity was based on cloth. Robert Watlington made his fortune from cloth and one of his sons, Samuel, built the house in 1688, on the site of an earlier building. The family lived there for over a century. In 1794, the house was leased to Edward Purvis, an army captain who fought in the Peninsular War. He died in 1820 and is said to haunt the building.

SAIL MAKING

Sail making was one branch of cloth making that survived until quite recently in Reading. It was made at the Oracle and in Katesgrove, and among their main customers were the East India Company and the Royal Navy. A number of the ships at the Battle of Trafalgar were carrying Reading sailcloth.

SAUCE

For over a century, Reading was perhaps as famous as Worcestershire for its sauce. James Cocks set up his Reading Sauce

Cock's Sauce factory, King's Road, around 1890.

NOTICE!

IN CONSEQUENCE OF THE MANY SPURIOUS
IMITATIONS OF

CHARLES COCKS'

ORIGINAL READING SAUCE,

Purchasers of this popular condiment (first introduced to the
public in 1789), are particularly requested to observe that the

on a white ground, is printed across the Reading Arms
on the Orange Coloured Label, without which NONE are
genuine.

ALSO

CHARLES COCKS'

ESSENCE OF ANCHOVIES,

Old England Sauce, Pickles, &c.

6, Duke Street, Reading.

A Cock's Sauce advertisement from 1867, warning against impersonations.

49

factory in 1789, operating from a warehouse in Duke Street. By 1814, his product was so well known that a London oil merchant called Mr Shout was fined 100 guineas for trying to counterfeit it. At the trial, it was said that Cock's Reading Sauce was sold at a hundred shops in London and in every major town in the United Kingdom. In later years, Cock's Sauce was made in a factory in King's Road, near to what is now Jackson's Corner.

SILK MAKING

Silk making came to prominence in Reading in the seventeenth and eighteenth centuries. It was encouraged by Queen Elizabeth I, who gave the town some mulberry trees to feed the silkworms. For many years a silk factory stood on the south side of the Abbey Gateway, and Huntley and Palmers' factory in King's Road was built on the site of a failed silk factory. About five hundred people were employed in silk making and related industries in 1809, out of a total town population of less than twelve thousand.

BRICK MAKING

Brick making was carried out in many parts of Reading from early in the town's history. There are records of a brick kiln at Emmer Green as early as 1654, which was in operation until quite recently. A local brick maker from Tilehurst supplied the builders of the Oracle in 1627. Katesgrove, Newtown, Whitley and Coley were also among the early brick-making areas of the town. The Rose Kilns, near to the River Kennet, gave their name to Rose Kiln Lane.

Reading's leading brick makers were S. and E. Collier. They moved from Coley to Grovelands in lower Tilehurst, where they continued in business until 1965. The Town Hall is just one of the Reading buildings using their products.

Another leading local firm was the Tilehurst Potteries, just off Kentwood Hill. It was founded by Samuel Wheeler, who moved the business from Coley to Tilehurst in 1895. Many famous buildings, including the prime minister's residence, Chequers, the Middle Temple and Sidney Sussex College, Cambridge are roofed with its products. At its height in the 1920s, two hundred staff were turning out twenty million hand-made tiles a year.

The ready availability of a variety of different types of brick gave rise to Reading's tradition of patterned brickwork. Reading's good rail communication also meant that it was easy to import an even wider range of bricks from other brick-making areas of the country. Colour variations were achieved by using different clays (for example, blue-grey gault clay gives yellow bricks) or by varying manufacturing methods (a reduction in oxygen flows to the kiln gives a metallic purple brick, while increased temperature gives dark blue 'flared headers').

Some of the best patterned brickwork buildings were erected between 1870 and 1900. Many good examples remain, often in residential streets. Look in particular at the Cardiff Road area, lower Caversham, Prospect Street, Katesgrove, Battle, the Field Road/Garnet Street area, Redlands, Newtown and the Whitley Street/Basingstoke Road area. The borough council is now trying to protect the best examples of older patterned brickwork buildings and to encourage its use in new buildings.

No brick making is carried on in Reading today, but one of the kilns remains, at Honey End Lane, near Prospect Park.

PHOTOGRAPHY

One business which had a short but important history in Reading was that of the photographic pioneer William Henry Fox Talbot. He opened a shop at 55 Baker Street (then called Russell Terrace) in the winter of 1843/4. He apparently chose Reading partly because it was a convenient point on the Great Western Railway between London and his home in Lacock in Wiltshire. In addition, the town's air was cleaner and rents were cheaper.

The newcomers caused great suspicion among the locals. The business was run by 'a foreigner' – Dutchman Nicholas Henneman. They were secretive about their work – often working in the dark – and Henneman always wore gloves to disguise his hands, stained from the photographic chemicals. The rumour grew that they were banknote forgers, due to the large quantities of paper they bought.

The business was never a great commercial success in Reading

London Street, 1845; another Fox Talbot photograph. In the centre is Lovejoy's Library, a meeting place for the literary and scientific establishment of the day which had a national reputation. The proprietor, George Lovejoy, was a fearless campaigner on local issues, whose claims to fame included trying to persuade Charles Dickens to stand as member of parliament for Reading. The imposing building with columns is the Literary, Scientific and Mechanics' Institute, built in 1843. It later became a Primitive Methodist chapel and, in the twentieth century, the Everyman Theatre. In its early days, Charles Dickens read extracts from his *Pickwick Papers* to audiences there. (Science Museum 462/65)

and in 1847 it was moved to Regent Street in London. However, while Fox Talbot and Henneman were in Reading, they produced some of the most important early books on photography. They were also responsible for a wonderful photographic record of the town. The house from which the business operated still stands.

Reading's Stately Homes

CAVERSHAM PARK

The history of the manor of Caversham goes back at least to Norman times, and possibly even to the Saxons. Walter Giffard, a relative of William the Conqueror, was given the manor of Caversham after the Conquest. At that time, the manor was probably no more than a hunting lodge, possibly nearer the river than the present building. In the year 1200, the manor passed to William, the Earl Marshall of England. He was one of the most powerful men in the kingdom, and was instrumental in getting King John to sign Magna Carta at Runnymede in 1215.

Henry III succeeded his father, King John, in 1216 at the age of just nine. For the next two years, William, who was now in his eighties, virtually ruled the country. When he knew he was dying, William asked to be brought from London to Caversham Park to end his days. The whole of the royal household came with him and William died there in May 1218.

Caversham Park was thereafter owned by some of the greatest names in the land – the Earls of Pembroke, Gloucester and of Warwick. In the fifteenth century it was the property of Warwick the Kingmaker and after his execution it became a Crown property. The estate gradually fell into disrepair.

It was in 1542 that the estate came into the possession of Sir Francis Knollys. His son William was comptroller of the royal household and he rebuilt the old house in a much grander style. Both Queen Elizabeth I and Queen Anne, consort of James I, stayed at the house.

When William Knollys died the estate passed to William, Lord Craven. He was an ardent supporter of Charles I and was rumoured to be the lover of Charles's sister, Queen Elizabeth of Bohemia. He paid for his support of the monarchy with the confiscation of all his property by the Parliamentarians. Caversham Park was bought by Lord George Vaux, who stripped the house for building materials and felled many of the trees in

Caversham Park, at the time of its occupation by the Marsack family.

the park for use by the navy. With the restoration of the monarchy, the Cravens had the ruins of their estate returned to them and it remained in their hands almost until the end of the seventeenth century.

The next owner of note, in 1718, was William Cadogan. He was a soldier who served under the Duke of Marlborough and went on to succeed him as general of the king's forces. His other titles included Viscount Caversham and Baron Cadogan of Reading. There seems to have been some friendly rivalry between him and the Duke of Marlborough. When Marlborough built the magnificent Blenheim Palace at Woodstock, Cadogan followed suit at Caversham Park, demolishing and redeveloping the old manor house. It cost him what was the then enormous sum of £130,000 and had a frontage of 300ft, only 20ft less than the garden facade at Blenheim.

Cadogan died in 1726 but the house remained in the family over half a century longer. His nephew, Charles Sloane Cadogan, brought in the great landscape architect Capability Brown, who removed all traces of the previous formal garden. Future American president Thomas Jefferson came to visit the gardens at Caversham Park in 1786. Some time during this period, the house was destroyed by fire and replaced with a much smaller residence.

In 1784, the estate was sold to Major Charles Marsack, who had recently retired from service in the Indian Army. A degree of mystery surrounded Major Marsack, who was alleged to be an illegitimate son of George II by the Comtesse de Marzac, a lady of Huguenot descent who came over with the Hanoverian court. Marsack carried out a number of improvements to this house, but his overbearing manner, high living and his felling of many fine trees in the park made him unpopular with local people.

Marsack was succeeded by his son, who sold off the house in 1838 to pay off his gambling debts. It was bought by William Crawshay, a wealthy ironmaster from Wales. In 1850, fire once again totally destroyed the house. Despite neither the house nor its contents being insured, Crawshay completely rebuilt it. This time the house was built around a steel frame and Crawshay took the precaution of buying his own fire engine. By the time Crawshay died in 1867 he had made a fortune from the building of the railways and was worth nearly £2 million. The house remained in the family until around 1920, when it was occupied by the Oratory RC School, founded by Cardinal Newman in

The great fire at Caversham Park, 1850, as shown in the *Illustrated London News* of the time. The scale of the home, which had been extended by the Crawshay family, can be seen.

1859 for upper-class Catholics. In 1943, the present owners, BBC Monitoring Services, took it over.

The grounds in which the house stands today are much smaller than they were in the past because large areas have been built on to form Caversham Park Village and parts of Emmer Green. When Caversham was taken into Reading in 1911, the Caversham Park estate was excluded, largely on the grounds that it would never be built upon! Caversham Park Village only became a part of Reading in 1977.

THE MANSION HOUSE

What we know today as the Mansion House is correctly called Prospect Hill House. The older part of the house was built on the site of an even older property, in 1759. The estate, which had once been owned by the Kendrick family (of Oracle fame) was at that time owned by Benjamin Childs. Childs had become lord of the manor of Tilehurst in 1706 and had married Frances Kendrick. She was the subject of a popular ballad called 'The

Berkshire Lady', which told the story of her securing a husband by challenging Childs either to fight a duel with her or to marry her.

The house that was built then was a fairly plain, rectangular, brick-faced building (essentially the central part of the house as we now know it). John Englebert Liebenrood bought the house in 1800 and greatly extended it. He added the east and west wings, the colonnaded portico and the bays on the main part, and had the whole building finished in stucco. Various further additions were made over the next hundred years. A *porte cochère* was added to the rear, so that carriages could drop off their occupants under cover, and a decorative verandah balcony was built.

The next owner of note was J.C. Fidler, a local businessman and pillar of the council. Fidler had built his father's fruit shop up into a major business and went on to be a company director with substantial interests in the City of London. He was responsible for the rebuilding of the east side of West Street, the construction of Market Arcade between Broad Street and Friar Street, the construction of Queen Victoria Street and, in 1901, the council's acquisition of Prospect Park. It was bought 'for the benefit of weary workers who, when at rest, need some open space where communion with nature may be established'.

The facilities of the Park were developed, but the Mansion House itself was relatively neglected. Refreshments and teas were sold from there until the 1950s, but it was mainly used for storage and changing accommodation. The building gradually fell into decay. During the 1980s, many attempts were made to secure the refurbishment of the Mansion House. The problem was always to find a use that would pay for its restoration without excluding the public from part of the Park. At last agreement was reached with a major catering and brewing company, and the building has now been restored to much of its former glory.

Reading gaol, before its modernization. The gateway was said to be modelled on the one in Warwick Castle.

Crime and Punishment

The earliest recorded prison in Reading was built as part of the Abbey. Three small rooms were built over the Abbey Gateway which was, at one time, attached to St Laurence's church. They were used to imprison monks guilty of ecclesiastical offences. It was called the Compter and survived until the early days of the nineteenth century. After the dissolution of the Abbey it was used for debtors and civil prisoners. Among those sent there were members of the public who failed to show due respect to the worthies of the corporation!

Another cell was built into the eastern end of Blagrave's Piazza, which was also built on to the south wall of St Laurence's church. This was known as 'The Hole' or alternatively as 'The Churchwarden's Pew'. The latter name stems from the time when an eighteenth-century churchwarden was locked up in there overnight for being drunk and disorderly. This cell, and the municipal stocks, pillory and ducking stool, were the responsibility of the head constable who lived in a house on the other side of the Compter gateway.

The gaol in Castle Street, where St Mary's church now stands, was in use from the latter years of the sixteenth century. The records for 1585 tell of a John Greenwode, who was 'pressed to death' while in captivity. This barbarous practice involved laying the prisoner down and piling weights on him until he either gave his captors the information required, or died.

The prisoners were kept chained and fettered in a subterranean dungeon. They had to provide for themselves and those without either friends or private means had to throw themselves on the mercy of the Poor Law. One potential source of income for them was a grating in the street, through which they could beg. Above it was written a poem by local poet John Merrick:

> Oh ye whose hours exempt from sorrow flow
> Behold the seat of pain and want and woe;
> Think, while your hands th'entreated alms extend
> That what to us ye give, to God you lend.

The keeper of the gaol was unsalaried and relied upon money extracted from the prisoners for his livelihood. In 1720 there were complaints that he was not only cruel but exorbitant. Prison rules and scales of charges were finally drawn up in 1731. They included the following: rent for a single bed 2s. 6d. per week. Two in a bed was 1s. 6d. a week each (and felons were not allowed to share a bed with debtors without the debtor's consent). Prisoners were allowed to send out for whatever food and drink they could afford. On leaving, they had to pay a leaving fee of 13s. 4d. to the gaolkeeper and 2s. 6d. to the turnkey.

Among those imprisoned in the gaol were religious dissenters, including John Bunyan, and those who had been impressed into the armed forces. When the prison reformer John Howard visited there in 1779 he found that the prison, with a capacity of twenty, contained eighteen felons and debtors and nineteen impressed men.

By the 1780s the gaol was in serious disrepair. It was decided to adapt the recently constructed house of correction at the eastern end of the Forbury as a new gaol. Robert Brettingham, the architect of the High Bridge in Duke Street, was brought in to oversee the conversion.

Meanwhile, the former Greyfriars church had been in use as a bridewell or house of correction since 1631. An early nineteenth century account tells of the state of the bridewell by that time. The roof had been removed to prevent it falling in and the centre of the church had become an open exercise yard, its floor green with moss and slime. An earth privy stood in the centre.

The side aisles had been roughly partitioned off into cells measuring about 14ft by 6ft. No light or air entered the cells, there was no heating even in winter and their only furniture was a bed of straw. No kitchen or washing water was provided and the diet was mainly bread and water. As the observer put it: 'The ingenuity of mankind, one would have supposed, could not have contrived a place so well adapted to reduce their fellow men below the condition of beasts.'

The treatment of prisoners was also brutal. In the early nineteenth century, an unemployed workman was sentenced to be whipped for stealing a loaf of bread. The keeper of the bridewell at that time, a man called Paradise, carried out the sentence with such enthusiasm that the unfortunate man died of his injuries.

These conditions survived into the second half of the nineteenth century, when the new county gaol at the Forbury became available. The bridewell was then converted back into a church. Meanwhile, the last prisoners were transferred from Castle Street to Forbury Road by 1796. This new gaol had included a gibbet (on the site where St James' Roman Catholic church stands today) carefully sited to allow large crowds a good view of the executions. A treadmill was also introduced in 1822, one of the first gaols to be so equipped. Thirty-two prisoners powered it and in a working day of ten hours each man climbed the equivalent of 13,300ft.

Watching the prisoners at their work became a favourite leisure activity for Reading people. At first, the treadmill was used to power a flour mill. Later it was attached to a simple friction brake, making the work not only exhausting but completely unproductive.

Numerous attempts to escape the gaol were made. One of the more ingenious of these, in 1799, would have involved burning the entire prison down! The other prisoners heard of this and decided that it was not entirely in their interests. The gaolkeeper was alerted and the attempt was foiled.

The new prison was not successful. It turned out to be too small and was jerry-built. In 1842, it was decided to build a new prison on the same site, to be based on the new model prison at Pentonville. Part of the cost was met by a bequest by one Augustus Schutz, who was 'deeply interested in the welfare of juvenile delinquents'. The architect appointed was Giles Gilbert Scott, whose other important buildings include the Home Office and the Albert Memorial. The cost of the construction rose from the original estimate of £24,000 to over £40,000 by the time it opened in July 1844. However, the *Illustrated London News* described it as 'architecturally, by far the greatest ornament to the town'. As originally built, there was a series of turrets around the walls, giving it the appearance of an ancient castle. These were only demolished in 1971.

A system of strict solitary confinement was employed. Prisoners were known only by their numbers. They had to keep silent on the few occasions when they came into contact with each other and had peaks on their caps, which they were supposed to pull down to prevent them even recognizing each other. However, prisoners got round this by developing an efficient system of sign language. One survival of this is the prison term 'snout' for tobacco, which was indicated by the prisoner touching his nose.

Public executions continued to draw large crowds until the last one took place on 14 March 1862. This sentence was not reserved for murderers. In 1800, there were 220 offences on the statute book carrying the death sentence, including the theft of property worth over 1s. Among those hanged at Reading were William Giles (passing forged £5 notes), James Castle (sheep stealing), Charles White (a horse thief) and John Carter (for robbery and taking part in agricultural riots).

Reading's most famous prisoner was, of course, Oscar Wilde. He was sentenced to two years' hard labour for homosexuality in 1895 and was moved to Reading from Wandsworth. The hard-line prison governor, Colonel Henry Isaacson, vowed to 'knock the nonsense out of Oscar Wilde'. Wilde left the prison in May 1897 and during his subsequent stay in France wrote *The Ballad of Reading Gaol*. The ballad is dedicated to the memory of Trooper Charles Thomas Wooldridge, who was hanged in Reading in 1896 for murdering his wife. In it, Wilde describes conditions in the gaol:

> *Each narrow cell in which we dwell,*
> *It is a foul and dark latrine,*
> *And the foetid breath of living death*
> *Chokes up each grated screen.*
> *And all, but lust, is turned to dust*
> *In humanity's machine.*

During the First World War the gaol was used for Irish and foreign internees. The conditions in which they were kept, including their rates of pay, were rather better than those of the front-line soldiers. Between the wars, the prison stood vacant and became derelict. In 1939, plans were drawn up to use the prison again for fifth columnists and enemy aliens. Instead it was used to rehouse borstal inmates whose previous accommodation had been bombed. It then became a military prison for the Canadian Army. After 1945 it was used for young adult offenders and then again as a borstal. The borstal was closed in 1969, following accusations of cruelty to inmates. The prison was refurbished in 1971 and brought back into its present use.

Street Scenes

Some of Reading's streets are recognizably the same as a hundred years ago, while others have been totally transformed.

Numbers 11–19 Castle Street, photographed by Fox Talbot in 1845. (Science Museum)

Looking down Cross Street towards Broad Street in 1887. One of the premises on the right is signed 'W. Fossett, Tripedresser – established 1833'.

Duke Street from High Bridge in about 1910. In the distance can be seen Jackson's Corner and the rooftops of St Laurence's church and the town hall.

Castle Street – a view up the hill in about 1890. The Horse and Jockey Inn can be seen on the north side. The inn dates from before 1699.

Christchurch from Whitley Street, in about 1905. The Whitley pump in the foreground was evidently a place for people to congregate. No doubt the lack of traffic made it a more comfortable place to meet than it would be today!

The Railways Come to Reading

The old Reading station buildings serve as a direct reminder of the days of broad gauge and Isambard Kingdom Brunel. They were built during the years of the broad gauge, in 1865–7, enlarging and remodelling the station Brunel himself built in 1840. The bricks used to build them showed how much the railways opened up trade with other parts of the country. They came, not from one of the many local brickworks, but from Coalbrookdale in Shropshire. The finial on top of the clock tower is a reminder of those found on the earliest semaphore railway signals.

Left to right, the Great Western Hotel, the South-eastern railway terminus and the GWR station, in about 1865. The picture shows how this area was built up out of the Thames floodplain.

Across the road from the station is possibly the world's earliest surviving railway hotel, the Great Western, which was built in 1844. The Italian detail of its styling is similar to that of the Royal Station Hotel in Slough, and it is thought that Brunel himself may have designed it. The hotel closed in 1972 and the building was converted for use as offices.

During the nineteenth century, the novelist W. M. Thackeray came to Reading by rail. Not knowing the town, he climbed into a cab and ordered the cabbie to drive him to the Great Western Hotel. The cabbie duly crossed the road and attempted to charge him 1s. 6d. for the privilege.

A railway from London to Bristol was first considered as early as 1824, but it was not until 1833 that the Great Western Railway Company was set up. The directors appointed Brunel as their engineer. Parliamentary approval was given for the railway in 1835, and within three years the line between Paddington and Maidenhead was open.

Between Maidenhead and Reading, Brunel faced a major engineering challenge – the Sonning Cutting. It was 2 miles long and up to 60ft deep, all of it dug by hand. As the work got further and further behind schedule, Brunel had as many as twelve hundred men and two hundred horses, all working in a sea of mud. Up to 7,800 cubic feet of spoil had to be shifted for every foot of track that was laid. Many navvies were injured or killed during its construction. Also of great concern to many Reading residents was the fact that the railway workers used to come into Reading and spend several days drunk, each time they were paid. Around this time, the corporation petitioned the House of Lords for stricter controls over the town's 194 pubs, to control the problem.

The railway age finally came to Reading in 1840. A party of directors made the first trial run to Paddington in just forty-five minutes and scheduled services started on 30 March of that year.

Just six days before the opening, a freak whirlwind struck Reading. It drowned two fishermen in the River Thames and ripped off a 4-ton section of the station roof. Henry West, a young man who was fixing the glazing of the roof at the time, was hurled to his death. He is buried in St Laurence's churchyard, where a memorial to him can be seen. Opponents of this new form of transport seized upon the accident as divine proof that railways were an instrument of the devil. (Users of an over-crowded Network South-East train in the 1990s may have some sympathy for this view.)

Sonning Cutting claimed further lives on Christmas Eve, 1841. At this time, third-class passengers travelled in converted open wagons in goods trains, which took up to nine hours to make the journey between London and Bristol. On this day, their train ran into an earth slip in Sonning Cutting. Some passengers were thrown from their open wagons, while others were crushed where they sat. In all, eight were killed and seventeen injured. The public inquiry into the tragedy led to the introduction of closed carriages for third-class passengers. However, these were virtually without windows or ventilation. By contrast, first-class compartments were modelled on the staterooms of river steamers and members of the nobility like the Duke of Wellington even took their own private coaches on special rail wagons. Second-class compartments had windows – but no glass! Deaths from exposure were recorded while travelling second class on the GWR.

Reading station was built on an embankment, to Brunel's controversial one-sided design. In this, both the up and down platforms were built on the south side of the same line, with a passing loop round the other platform (see Figure 1 overleaf). The platforms were separate, each with its own booking office, and there was another line for non-stopping trains to pass through the station.

Brunel did this for the convenience of his passengers, since virtually all of Reading was on the south side of the station. But it proved to be a very dangerous method of operation on occasion. In one incident, a non-stop express train was mistaken by the pointsman as a stopping train. He switched the points and the express went thundering into the station at 55 mph. By a miracle, the passengers escaped with a severe shaking and their baggage scattered from the tops of the wagons on to the platform. The pointsman was found, still clutching his lever, standing bolt upright in a dead faint!

Reading acquired a second station in 1849, when the South-Eastern Railway was connected to the town. Until its closure in 1965, the terminus stood on what is now the site of the new station concourse.

From its early days, the inadequacy of Reading's station was a source of complaint for the local townspeople. The Great Western Railway Company was deaf to their calls for improvements, until a derailed goods wagon forced the issue in 1853. It crashed into the columns of the station and brought the roof down. Even so, it was not until 1896 that the old system of single platform

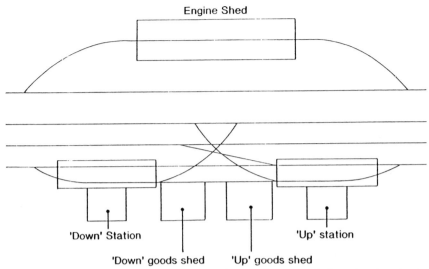

Figure 1: Simplified view of the layout of Brunel's one-sided station (c. 1849)

working came to an end and the company began installing the modern ten platforms.

Another major rail accident occured on 12 September 1855, when a pilot engine was signalled out on to the wrong line. It collided head-on with the 4.40 train from London, killing three passengers and injuring many others.

Brunel built his railways on the 7′ 0″ broad gauge, but the 4′ 8½″ gauge gradually became accepted as the national standard. By 1861, standard-gauge lines had been laid between Paddington and Reading. However, standard-gauge trains could not use the existing platforms. New platforms had to be built, at the outer ends of the existing platforms. This could have meant Reading station ending up with no less than four booking offices. Instead, the Great Western Railway eventually built the station building we see today.

Although the railways dramatically cut journey times to London, the fares were not particularly cheap for the average person. In 1880, a standard return fare to London would have cost 8s. 3d., while first-class travel cost 11s. 8d.

Today, Reading is still one of the most important railway junctions on Network South-East, with direct links to many parts of the country.

The last broad-gauge train passes through Reading in May 1892.

The up station and railway lines in about 1890.

Beer, Biscuits and Bulbs

The foundation of Reading's economic success in the nineteenth century was beer, biscuits and bulbs.

SIMONDS BREWERY

One thing Reading has never been short of is public houses. In 1700 the town had 104 pubs to serve a population of under 8,000. By the middle of the nineteenth century, 21 breweries were supplying over 200 pubs, at a time when around 25,000 people lived in the town.

By far the most successful of these was founded in Broad Street by William Simonds in 1785. He rapidly expanded and in 1790 moved to Bridge Street. His new brewery was built on the site of a dyeing house that dated back to 1221. There he also built a family home, Seven Bridges House, that survives to this day. The eminent architect was Sir John Soane, who was born near Reading and whose other works include the Bank of England.

Simonds made his fortune by taking advantage of a change in the law and becoming one of the first brewers to supply the wholesale trade. A further piece of good business was his decision to supply free beer to troops exercising on Salisbury Plain. This brought him a huge order from the army.

By 1799, Simonds's business had flourished enough for him to lease Caversham Court, a riverside mansion next to St Peter's church in Caversham. Even at home his business acumen did not fail him. He made a good deal of money from the chalk pits in the garden of his house, turning it into a substantial mining operation. He also had most of the old Tudor house demolished and replaced by one designed by the famous architect, Augustus Welby Pugin (of Houses of Parliament fame). The house remained in the family until 1909 and was finally demolished in 1933.

Meanwhile, Simonds's Brewery flourished until it became part

year. 1924

Simonds Brewery. A steam delivery wagon dating from 1924.

of the Courage empire in 1960. By then, it had expanded its manufacturing on to a huge site on either side of Bridge Street. In 1973, plans were announced to move to a new 70-acre site at Worton Grange, next to the motorway. Thus, almost two hundred years of brewing at Bridge Street came to an end in 1980.

Simonds also diversified into banking. The ornate Italianate bank building on King Street, now occupied by Barclays, was built for Simonds Bank in 1836. Their name is still on the front door. From early in the nineteenth century Simonds Bank was issuing its own £1 notes.

One thing does not change – people will always complain about the quality of the beer. As one visitor to Reading put it in 1810: 'Though I cannot say much in praise of their beer, I think it is as good as the most skilful modern chymist could brew without malt or hops.' Whether or not he was referring to Mr Simonds's brews we shall never know!

HUNTLEY AND PALMERS

Hannah Huntley, wife of the headmaster of a school in Burford, Oxfordshire, baked biscuits in the school oven. She sold them outside the school gate, where the coaches stopped. Her elder stepson, Joseph, moved to Reading in 1811 and eleven years later began selling biscuits from a shop at 72 London Street. His son, Thomas, did the baking. Again their market was travellers stopping at the Crown Inn, opposite.

One of the main problems with biscuits at this time was that it was difficult to keep them fresh while they were being transported. The only 'portable' biscuit was the disgusting object issued to the armed forces which was usually full of weevils and had to be broken with a chisel! The solution to this problem was to be found next door to the Crown Inn, where Joseph's younger son worked as an ironmonger. Huntley had them make some small tin-plate boxes to store biscuits. This was the start of Huntley, Boorne and Stevens, whose decorative tins were used to send Huntley and Palmers' biscuits all round the world.

Joseph Huntley retired because of ill-health in 1838 and his son Thomas took over. As the market for biscuits grew, George Palmer joined Huntley in partnership in 1841. Palmer introduced ideas for the mass production of biscuits and the scene was set for large-scale expansion. By 1851 the new factory at

A ceramic plaque, advertising Huntley and Palmers, and showing their factory.

King's Road was opened, employing two hundred people. Ten years later, employees numbered four hundred; by 1868 there were a thousand, and by the outbreak of the First World War, six thousand.

The factory expanded on to both sides of the Kennet, with the old factory site serving the home market and the new one on the site of the old Blake's Wharf producing biscuits for export. Thomas Huntley died in 1857, ten years before the company was given the honour of being allowed to describe itself as 'By appointment to Her Majesty the Queen'. Osborne biscuits were named after Queen Victoria's residence in the Isle of White.

Huntley and Palmers' biscuits became famous the world over. When the first British expedition to Tibet reached the capital, Lhasa, they found tins of biscuits in the Dalai Lama's palace. No European had ever been to Lhasa before. Explorers in the jungles of New Guinea found a native chief wearing a Huntley and Palmers' biscuit tin lid on a cord around his neck, like a medal.

Biscuit manufacture continued at King's Road until 1977. For a time, Nabisco (who took over Huntley and Palmers) kept their administrative centre there. This closed recently and the main building has been redeveloped.

Many other traces of Huntley and Palmers presence in the town remain. George Palmer's house at 44 London Road became part of the original university complex. But most of all the Palmer family will be remembered for their generosity to the town. They acquired part of King's Meadow for the town. They provided model homes for their workforce, including the estate built in 1876 at the Mount. They met part of the cost of the town hall complex and provided the land and part of the cost of the buildings for the university. Not least, they provided the park which bears George Palmer's name. His statue, which used to be in the middle of Broad Street, is now in the Park.

SUTTONS SEEDS

John Sutton set up a corn and seed merchant's business in Reading in 1807. It might have remained a small local business, but for the business acumen of his son, Martin Hope Sutton. He began selling seeds on his own account in 1828, at the age of thirteen. In the 1830s Martin Sutton opened a trial seed ground

Suttons premises in Market Place, decorated for the coronation of Queen Elizabeth II in 1953.

which attracted great interest and admiration and in 1836, aged twenty-one, he became a partner in his father's business.

The firm was known as the Royal Seed Establishment from its earliest days. This stemmed from a business relationship established between John Sutton and the bailiff of the royal home farm at Windsor.

Suttons soon developed a reputation as honest traders in a profession which was at that time not noted for its reliability. Their advice was sought by the government in 1845, when the potato famine gripped Ireland. They supplied vegetable seed to replace the lost potato crop and helped to prevent the tragedy from becoming worse.

Martin Sutton began sending out free catalogues of their ever-expanding range of goods. The company also produced new and improved selections of seed and introduced strict standards of germination testing.

One of their more notable early clients was the Marquis of Granby, who spent a small fortune creating an ornamental park in the 80 acres of the Whiteknights estate.

The original premises for the business were on the eastern side of Market Place, close to the street market that drew farming people into the town each week. To the rear of the premises they had a garden, originally one of the gardens of the Abbey, which was used to display their products. By the 1920s the business had expanded enormously to cover much of the area between the Market Place, the Forbury, Abbey Street and King's Road. They also had extensive trial grounds, next to the railway on the edge of town.

The Sutton family were active in the life of the town. At least one member of the family, Martin John Sutton, became the town's mayor. Another Sutton, Herbert, helped in 1893 to establish the University Extension College which was later to grow into Reading University.

Suttons moved out of Reading in 1974, to Torquay. Little sign remains today of their business in the town. Their trial ground is now occupied by the Suttons Industrial Park and much of the Royal Seed Establishment has been redeveloped. However, some of the family's homes still survive. Hillside on Allcroft Road was occupied by the Sutton family (as well as by the Palmers) and Rosehill House in Caversham was once the home of Martin John Sutton.

Seats of Learning

READING SCHOOL

There is evidence to suggest that education of some description was going on in Reading in the year 1120, the year before the foundation of the Abbey. However, to try and link Reading School with this would be difficult in the extreme. A more reliable date for its foundation would be 29 March 1125. This was the day on which the foundation charter for Reading Abbey was signed and sealed at Rouen. This gave the abbot authority to carry on a variety of religious and secular activities, including education. If this date is accepted as the beginning of Reading School, that would make it the tenth oldest school in England.

Details of its early years are sketchy. There are records of one Radulfo de Gorges, a member of the king's household, being sent there for his education in 1246. It is also clear that the master of the school was already being woefully underpaid – something that was to be a recurring feature of the school's history. The accounts for 1345/6 show the annual cost of the master's stipend at just 3s. 4d.

In around 1465, the Hospitium of Reading Abbey closed. One of its original purposes – accommodating pilgrims – had been abandoned due to the decline in the popularity of pilgrimages. There were also charges of 'certain immoralities' against some of its residents.

The school in the Abbey had become more of a boarding school, moving away from the original objective of educating the poor children of the town. Abbot John Thorne decided in 1486 to take the opportunity to reform the school and house it in the Hospitium. It is said that Henry VII learned of these plans on a visit to Reading in that year and endowed the school with £10 a year from Crown rents collected in the town. However, there appears to be no documentary evidence to support this story. What is clear is that it took a number of years before the school had raised enough endowments to pay for its new role.

One of the first masters of the school, appointed in 1530, was Leonard Cockes. He was a friend of Erasmus and of Hugh Faringdon, Abbot of Reading, which was a dangerous thing to be at the time of the dissolution of the monasteries. In 1539, he entered into a covenant with Hugh Faringdon to ensure the future teaching of 'the Catholic faith piously and in an orthodox manner'. Despite this, Cockes survived and even prospered under Henry VIII. In 1541, the king granted Cockes the school and its mastership for life, paying him a salary of £10 a year from Crown rents.

Less fortunate was Julius (or Joceline) Palmer. Despite being a devout Catholic, he was made tutor to the sons of Sir Francis Knollys, who was well-known as a persecutor of papists. When the Catholic Mary Tudor came to the throne, Knollys took the wise precaution of fleeing abroad. Shortly after, Palmer became master of Reading School.

Palmer saw the Protestant martyrs Latimer and Ridley die. Despite his own religious leanings, he was appalled at their barbaric treatment and wrote a paper on the subject which was seized upon by his enemies. Palmer sold up and fled, but made the fatal mistake of returning to Reading to collect some of his belongings. While dining in the Cardinal's Hat Inn, he was betrayed to the mayor of Reading and arrested. He was found guilty of heresy at Newbury on 16 July 1555 and burnt at the stake the following day. Palmer was just twenty-four years old.

The 1560 charter granted by Queen Elizabeth I transferred the responsibility for hiring and firing (and, equally important, paying) the master of Reading School to the corporation. She did, however, endow the corporation with Crown rents to cover the cost of this, which was to be the basis on which the school was run for the next three hundred years.

Despite the charter, the corporation was by no means free of outside interference in running the school. Both William Laud and Oliver Cromwell took it upon themselves to dictate the choice of master. During the Civil War, the school was used as a gunpowder store and the master, William Page, had to flee the town to avoid arrest. For the next twenty years, the mastership of Reading School was to be a political and religious football. Cromwell's appointee was summarily sacked by the corporation, just as soon as Cromwell's son Richard fell from grace.

During the eighteenth century, the school gradually gained more pupils and more prestige. There was, however, conflict

The martyrdom of Julius Palmer, former master of Reading School, at the Sandpits near Newbury in 1555.

between town and school. One of the masters, John Spicer, tried to exclude the public from part of the Forbury, which doubled as the school playground and a public area. The townspeople retaliated by occupying the area with a cricket match. Spicer was forced to concede.

The school went into something of a decline before its most famous master, Doctor Valpy, was appointed in 1781. His career is set out elsewhere in this book (see p. 164). His son, who succeeded him as master, was not of the same calibre. Numbers declined from a peak of two hundred pupils to a point where an inspector found only two enrolled pupils, of whom 'one was absent and the other not there'!

In 1867, the mayor of Reading, Henry John Simonds, got an Act of Parliament passed to reconstitute the school under a new system of management. The new trustees included the mayor, aldermen and the vicars of the three parishes. They paid £4,000 for a 10-acre site from the Redlands Estate Company and designs for a new school building were drawn up by the architect Alfred Waterhouse. Once again, the Palmer family proved to be bene-factors of Reading, providing a loan of £6,000 towards the building costs. The council, by contrast, refused any further subsidy.

The purpose of the school was to prove controversial in the latter part of the nineteenth century. Was it supposed to be a centre of excellence, serving a fee-paying élite, or was it sup-posed to be serving purely local needs? People had violently differing views on the matter, and some sought an uneasy compromise between the two. The 1870 prospectus referred to 'a thorough Middle Class education to be supplemented by a lower school for the benefit of the lower classes'.

The head of the school at this time, Dr Thomas Stokoe, resigned in 1877, having given up any hope of raising the school to a recognized and important position among the first grade of public schools. The controversy about the nature and future of the school led to a long correspondence in The Times and attracted the involvement of the Charity Commissioners. They made the trustees draw up a clear plan for the school. Mean-while, in 1877, the Berkshire Chronicle objected to the principle of rateborne subsidy for the school. 'Do they mean', (the paper asked, 'that the denizens of Silver Street [the poorest street in the borough] are to pay for the education of boys who live in the best houses in the town and neighbourhood?'

Reading School. A painting by Herbert Beecroft, dating from 1898.

The school was suffering from a financial crisis, as well as a crisis of identity. Under the 1867 Act, the council became responsible if the trustees defaulted on their mortgages. This happened, and from 1886 the council was picking up part of the bill for running the school, without having any direct influence over its activities. This unsatisfactory situation was resolved in 1908, when the council took over the running of the school. Today, the school is still part of the state sector, but receives its funding direct from central government.

KENDRICK SCHOOL

Kendrick School has its origins in the Kendrick charities which, among other things, had established the Oracle. A small part of these charities had been preserved for the borough after the Oracle had been demolished. In 1877, these were used to establish schools for a hundred boys and a hundred girls. The boys' school was in a new building in King's Road, while the girls' school was in Watlington House.

Again, there was controversy about the purpose of the schools.

Although scholarships were to be awarded on merit, the Reading Working Men's Liberal Association objected to the fact that the changed purpose of the charity would transfer money intended for the poor to the middle classes.

Kendrick Boys' School was amalgamated into Reading School in 1915. After many years of negotiation, Kendrick Girls' School was able to move out of its crowded accommodation in Watlington Street. New purpose-built accommodation was provided for it next to Mary Russell Mitford's house, on the corner of London Road and Sidmouth Street, in 1927.

BLUECOAT SCHOOL

Richard Aldworth was a merchant who made his fortune in Reading and London. In 1646, he made a gift of £4,000 to found a boarding school for 'twenty poor boys'. He was a governor of Christ's Hospital, where the original Blue Coat School was founded, and he decreed that the uniform of the Reading institution should be similar to it. For many years, the school occupied premises at the corner of Silver Street and London Street. Only in 1946 did it move to Holme Park in Sonning.

One of its more interesting former pupils is one Seth Wisdom, who made a fortune from selling false teeth which fitted over one's existing teeth without the need for extractions! He retired to a mansion at Victoria Square, on King's Road, where the technical college now stands.

Reading's Town Halls

Reading has a long and chequered history of local government. The first charter giving the town powers of self-government was granted in 1253. There were even stories of older powers, dating back to the time of Edward the Confessor, but no such charter has ever been found.

Four of the buildings which have provided a home for local government in Reading still stand today. The first recorded home of the corporation was on the banks of the Kennet, near to the site of the High Bridge on Duke Street. The yield hall, from which Yield Hall Place takes its name, was recorded as being in use in 1420. Its major drawback was that it was right next door to the town's communal washing place – the launderette of its day. The records show that council meetings were drowned out by the noise of housewives on the river bank, beating their washing with wooden implements to get the dirt out. Parts of this yield hall survived into the 1920s.

Just after the dissolution of the monasteries, in 1543, the council took over the nave of Greyfriars church as their guild-hall. The old yield hall passed into private hands – part of it was rented out as 'hogstyes'! By 1578, Greyfriars was being used as a hospital cum workhouse for the poor. Shortly afterwards, parts of it were converted into a house of correction for the idle and vagrant. Around this time the council moved again. The ground floor of the refectory in the former Abbey Hospitium had been used as the school room of Reading School since 1487. The council put a new upper storey into the building for its own use.

By this time, an important new charter had been granted to the town, by Queen Elizabeth I in 1560. This increased the powers of the corporation, giving it the right to own land, to run markets and fairs, responsibilities for consumer protection, the maintenance of a prison and powers to appoint or dismiss the master of Reading School.

Although it lasted for some two hundred years, the new town hall was far from ideal. The council chamber was split in two by a row of heavy pillars. This made the room most unsuitable for large meetings. When the assizes were held there, two separate courts operated in the same room, with only a curtain between them. The confusion this caused is described by a contemporary observer: the courts were 'so contrived that, while from the usual echo of a large room you are prevented from hearing the evidence in that wherein you are sitting, you may, without moving from your situation, derive amusement from the pleadings of the counsel in the other'. Moreover, the redoubtable Dr Valpy, master of Reading School, found the noise of council business above his head so disruptive that he had a new school building erected at his own expense. By the 1780s, the building was also showing signs of structural failure.

In 1785/6, this building was taken down and replaced, at a cost of £1,800, with a new hall. This was designed by Alderman Charles Poulton, who was a cabinet-maker rather than an architect. This building survives today, as the Victoria Hall – part of the beautifully restored town hall complex. It has seen many distinguished visitors over the years. Among them was Charles Dickens, who came there on three occasions to give readings of his work.

By the latter part of the nineteenth century the role of local government had grown. More space was needed. A local architect who had developed a national reputation was brought in to design it. Alfred Waterhouse was the son of a Liverpool Quaker family. He moved to Reading in 1870. He built his own house, Foxhill, on the Whiteknights estate. His track record with local government buildings was an impressive one. A few years before, he had designed what was at the time one of the world's grandest, and certainly most expensive, buildings, Manchester Town Hall.

The buildings were completed over almost a quarter of a century, by three different architects. Waterhouse's first phase was finished in 1875. The second phase, containing the public library and museum, opened in 1882. The architect this time was Thomas Lainson. His appointment caused a controversy among architects. When Waterhouse's designs for phase two proved too expensive, a competition was organized to choose an alternative. Lainson was appointed to assess the entrants, and managed to get himself appointed to do the job! Yet another architect, W.R. Howell, designed the library extension and the art gallery at the Valpy Street end. This opened in 1897. These last two phases were largely paid for by public subscription. As with many other improvements to the town at this time, the Palmer

The Old Town Hall in about 1880, before the second and third phases were built.

family underwrote much of the cost. Sir Francis Goldsmid was another of the major benefactors.

A local brick maker, S. and E. Collier of Tilehurst, supplied the brick and terracotta mouldings for the buildings. The mouldings show scenes from Reading's history and you can see that the architect for phase two failed to get a perfect match for the grey bricks Waterhouse used in his first phase. Possibly, years of smoke had already stained phase one, leading him to choose the darker, Staffordshire blue brickwork – a problem that only emerged when the whole building was cleaned.

The Town Hall contains one feature of international importance – its organ, which was originally built for the little town hall in 1864 and moved into the Great Hall in 1882. The mid-nineteenth century was a golden age for British organ building and 'Father' Henry Willis, who built the Reading organ, was the greatest of Victorian organ builders. Other examples of his work are to be found in the Royal Albert Hall and many of our great cathedrals, including Canterbury, Salisbury, Durham and St Paul's. Reading's organ is especially important, being the least changed of his major works.

Its history has not been without controversy. Its inaugural concert in 1864 was a complete shambles. The instrument had not been properly finished and ticket prices had to be reduced. When the guest organist tried to play it, all he could get out of it was a faint wheeze – the weight of the crowded audience had caused the floor to bow, constricting the air supply to the organ. Only desperate work by Father Willis on the night got the instrument half-way playable by the end of the evening. However, over the years, the qualities of the instrument have come to be recognized world-wide. They are helped not a little by the almost perfect acoustics of the Great Hall, designed by Thomas Lainson without the benefits of modern acoustic science.

The museum displays were built around the collection of Horatio Bland, a nineteenth-century traveller. He appears to have been a compulsive collector, and sometimes one of slightly dubious taste. The collection he presented to the council included a decorated cider jar from Ecuador (6 ft in circumference!), bricks from the walls of Babylon, the head and hands of a mummy, taken personally by him from a pyramid, an opium pipe, specimens of compressed fish and the skeleton of a boa constrictor. Reading people added to this bizarre collection with enthusiasm. Attics were cleared out and the council was deluged with stuffed crocodiles and other curiosities.

The council rapidly outgrew these premises. As early as 1901, the council resolved to concentrate all the civic buildings, including the police station and magistrates' courts, on a single site. Plans to extend the town hall complex on its existing site were interrupted by the First World War. After the war, a variety of options were suggested, including the north-west corner of the Forbury Gardens (which was rightly rejected after a public outcry), Hills Meadow, the prison site at Forbury Road (at that time disused), Prospect Park and an area off London Road, near Sidmouth Street. The Hosier Street site became available due to slum clearance after the Second World War. But even then there was a long debate about whether or not to sell the site for commercial offices. Thus it was not until 1976, three-quarters of a century after the need for them was identified, that the present civic offices were opened.

The mayor-elect of Reading in 1862, John Okey Taylor, said, 'It takes three centuries to carry anything out in Reading: one to think about it, one to talk about it, and another to carry it out.' In the case of Reading's new civic offices, he was not far wrong.

Reading University and Whiteknights

Although Reading's university is a twentieth-century creation, Reading almost became a major university town several hundreds of years earlier.

Until the twelfth century, wealthy families sent their children to study at the University of Paris. Wars with the French put an end to that and people began to turn instead to the Grey Friars at Oxford, who had established a centre of learning. As it evolved into a university, antagonism grew up between the students and the Jewish community in Oxford. Many of the latter had gained wealth and influence as landlords of student accommodation. This erupted into sporadic violence over the years, but in 1355 widespread disorder broke out. Many people were brutally murdered, houses were looted and fires were started. At one point, the river was ablaze with flaming oil from a nearby storehouse. The violence multiplied, as the poor of the city went to the support of the burgesses, many of whom were also Jewish landlords.

The friars attempted to restore order, but were fallen upon by bloodthirsty townspeople. A massacre of horrifying viciousness followed and those scholars who survived fled the city. A few of them made their way to Cambridge, where they provided the nucleus of a new university. The majority came to join their fellow Franciscans in Reading. They tried to set up a seat of learning in Reading, but without success. The people of Reading were more interested in what they could make from the Grey Friars than what they could learn. Gradually they drifted back to by-now peaceful Oxford. Reading had to wait until the Victorians sowed the seeds of the modern university.

The Whiteknights estate has a long and chequered history, and the name itself is linked to a legend. Gilbert de Montalieu was the son of a close friend of William the Conqueror. It is said that he was made governor of Reading and fell in love with Editha, the daughter of a Saxon king. When he found her kissing another Saxon, he killed the man. He learned later that the murdered man was Editha's brother. Editha, grief-stricken, entered a convent and Gilbert went on a long penance to Jerusalem. Many years later, the body of an elderly white knight was found lying on the grave of Editha's brother. It was Gilbert, and the grave is supposed to lie close to the Wokingham Road entrance to the Whiteknights estate.

By the sixteenth century, the estate belonged to the Englefield family. Staunchly Catholic, Sir Francis Englefield had a turbulent career during the religious upheavals of the times. He was imprisoned for his faith in 1551, made master of the Court of Wards and Liveries under the Catholic Queen Mary, then forced to flee the country in 1558 when Queen Elizabeth ascended to the throne. His lands were forfeit to the Crown in 1585, but his family bought them back in 1606.

They remained in the Englefield family until 1783. Shortly after, in 1798, they came into the ownership of George Spencer Churchill, Marquis of Blandford and an ancestor of Winston Churchill. Over the next twenty years, he spent a small fortune creating landscaped gardens on the estate, collecting old masters and building up a library of rare books. Local people were allowed to use the estate, subject to certain conditions. On one occasion, William Blandy, a member of a long-established and influential local family, found the gates to the estate locked. He threatened to bring a man with a sledgehammer to open them! This had the desired effect upon the gatekeeper.

The marquis's extravagance bankrupted him by 1819, two years after becoming Duke of Marlborough. He sold up and the house, after standing empty for a number of years, was demolished in 1840. In about 1849, the estate passed to Sir Isaac Goldsmid, a wealthy bullion broker. His son, Francis, was to become the member of parliament for Reading from 1860 until his death in a rail accident in 1878. They divided the estate up into six parts. One of the plots, Foxhill, was where Alfred Waterhouse built his house. It was later occupied by Lord Hirst, founder of the giant General Electric Company. The estate remained in the Goldsmid family until the university acquired it with the help of a government grant.

The university had its origins in art classes, started in 1860, under the auspices of the Department of Science and Art at the museums at South Kensington. Classes were held in various

University College, Valpy Street, in 1899. The old Hospitium of Reading Abbey.

parts of the town and their popularity grew rapidly. It was Herbert Sutton, of the Sutton's Seeds family, who subsidized the setting up of a university college in 1893. He bought the vicarage next to St Laurence's church and let it to the college at a nominal rent.

The University College, as it had by then become, outgrew the vicarage by 1904. Alfred Palmer endowed it with 6 acres of land at London Road and a building fund of £50,000. In 1906, the future secretary for war, Richard Haldane, opened the new campus. The Palmer family and Lady Wantage (after whom Wantage Hall is named) created a £200,000 endowment fund for its further development.

During the First World War, the college was taken over by the Royal Flying Corps and trainee munition workers. Studies resumed after the war and in 1926 it finally became a fully-fledged university. The 300-acre Whiteknights estate was bought by the university in 1947, but the transfer of activities from London Road to the campus has still to be completed after forty years.

The Victorian Building Boom – King's Road and Queen's Road

The Reading that we know today is still essentially a Victorian creation. In the period of Victoria's reign the town grew from around eighteen thousand people to one which had almost eighty thousand within its enlarged boundaries. Many of the major institutions of the town were established in this period.

Reading owed its rapid growth to two related factors. One was the expansion of local industries, discussed earlier. The second factor was the growth of the railways, which carried the products of Reading manufacturers to every corner of the country.

An important stimulus to the development of the town was the construction of King's Road in 1832, across land which had been in the ownership of the Crown since the dissolution of the Abbey. This created a new and more direct route eastwards from the town centre, opening up the whole of the area between Duke Street and Cemetery Junction for development. The Crown estate in this area was shortly afterwards sold by auction, as was the corporation's land in the area of Queen's Road, South Street and Sidmouth Street.

In the event, King's Road never became the high road to London. Within less than ten years it had been overtaken by the coming of the railways. Development took place, none the less. Shops, warehouses and factories grew up around the canal while, further to the east, areas of attractive villas were developed to serve the growing staff of the newly opened Royal Berkshire Hospital nearby.

ROYAL BERKSHIRE HOSPITAL

Until the beginning of the nineteenth century, the ordinary people of Reading had no proper medical care. It was in 1802 that the Reading Dispensary began providing a very basic service of dispensing medicines to the poorer people of the town. However, it was an uphill battle against the poverty and poor sanitation that existed at the time. By the 1870s, about one-third of the population of Reading were members of the Dispensary, many of them paying a small weekly sum for medicine and advice.

The existence of the Royal Berkshire Hospital is largely due to the persistence of a retired bank clerk called Richard Oliver. He fought a long and determined campaign to provide a new hospital 'suitable for a town whose dignity may appear to be irretrievably lost in squalor but which can be captured by the united efforts of its citizens'. Oliver lobbied everyone from King William IV (who is the 'Royal' in the title) downwards in his campaign. He used the royal connection to persuade the former prime minister Lord Sidmouth to donate the land, on which the hospital was built by public subscription. This was despite the objections of Lady Sidmouth, who found the idea of a hospital on her land 'very objectionable'.

She was not alone in her opposition. There were even those, incredibly, who argued against providing a hospital at all, on the grounds that it would attract 'delicate and sick people' to the town. But Oliver's persistence paid off and on 27 May 1839 a grand procession led by five hundred Sunday school children marked the opening of the hospital.

Royal Berkshire Hospital.

The building that was opened in 1839 still stands, fronting on to London Road. Designed by local architect Henry Briant, it was extended during the rest of the nineteenth century, but the extensions blend in well with the original.

The first patient to be treated was George Earley, a fifteen-year-old labourer who lost his arm, building the Sonning Cutting section of the Great Western Railway. The directors of the railway were persuaded (with how much difficulty one does not know) to make a contribution towards the hospital's costs, because of the amount of custom they provided during the building of the line to Bristol.

The need for the hospital was soon proved by the rate at which it grew. From its initial sixty beds, it doubled in size by 1866 and was soon expanding further. In 1867 the whole system of nursing was changed. The old nurses apparently performed their duties 'in a matter of fact manner that jarred painfully on the sensitive nerves of a patient, and not infrequently retarded the progress of recovery'. Teaching of staff thereafter became an important part of nursing in the hospital, something which continues today.

In its first year, the hospital treated 304 in-patients and 274 out-patients. This rose by 1878 to 1,079 in-patients and 1,620 out-patients. Just like hospitals today it had its financial problems, and was losing around £700 a year by the 1870s. This shortfall was made up by a collection in all the local churches, which raised £1,100 in 1878.

Richard Oliver, the original champion of the hospital, ended his days there. He was knocked down by a horse-drawn Huntley and Palmers' wagon in London Street in 1855 and died in Benyon Ward.

The hospital received unexpected royal patronage in 1871. The Prince of Wales, travelling to Reading to open the new Reading School buildings, got some grit in his eye. The royal coach was diverted from its expected route into the hospital, giving rise to rumours of his terminal illness and death among the watching crowds!

REDLANDS

The Redlands estate has a history going back to Saxon times. Its name was derived from the Saxon name for the Reading to Shinfield Road, Rudden Lane. At various times it belonged to

Reading Abbey, the Blagrave family and to Sir Francis Knollys, whose accomplishments included adventuring and piracy with Sir Francis Drake. Lord Sidmouth sold off 126 acres of the estate for housing in 1865. Part of it was acquired as the new site for Reading School and 4 acres of it were bought by Alfred Sutton. He built his new home, Greenlands, on the site. Much of it was acquired by the Redlands Estate Company, founded by local chemist Peter Spokes, who divided it up into building plots. Two of the streets are named after Richard Benyon de Beauvoir and Lord Carnarvon, both of whom were major subscribers to the Royal Berkshire Hospital and had their names preserved for posterity in return.

The Marquis of Granby is one of the most historic inns in the area. It was originally called the Gallows Tavern, after the nearby gallows, but was renamed after the commander-in-chief of the British Army during the Seven Years' War, who owned the nearby Whiteknights estate.

FORBURY GARDENS

The Forbury Gardens were originally the outer court of the Abbey. Following the dissolution, the rest of the Abbey lands were sold off, but the people retained the right to hold fairs and public events there. Many of the most important events in the history of the town were celebrated in this area.

The area was not always the attractive park we know today. In the early nineteenth century it was the site of a dung heap formed by the town's scavenger, so high that it blocked out the views across to south Oxfordshire. The rest of the town's population used it as a rubbish dump.

Various attempts were made over the years to improve the Forbury Gardens, some as a means of keeping unemployed men off parish relief. Joshua Vines, a resident of Friar Street, oversaw improvements to Forbury Hill in 1831, but it was not until 1855 that the council acquired part of the area and laid it out as gardens at a cost of £1,350. The Gardens were further extended in 1861 and 1871, at the same time as the Abbey ruins were being tidied up.

The statue of the Maiwand Lion, often used as a symbol of Reading, was added in 1886. It commemorates the death of 328 officers and men of the Royal Berkshire Regiment at Maiwand, in the Afghan Wars of 1879/80. They fought a valiant rearguard action that allowed their comrades to escape.

PUBLIC SERVICES

It was during this period that many of the public services we take for granted today also came into being.

Police

The first borough police force was set up in 1836. They took over from the nightwatchmen appointed by the commissioners for paving. The original force consisted of thirty constables, two sergeants and two inspectors and their police station was at 6 Friar Street. No women were appointed to the police force until 1917, but even then they did not get powers to arrest anyone until 1941!

Fire brigade

The Watch Committee acquired two fire engines in 1844, but a separate fire brigade was not established until 1862. By 1880 they had two fire engines and a fire escape, which they kept in a yard at the police station. Both Huntley and Palmers' and Suttons had their own independent fire brigades, as did some local insurance companies. The fire service became a separate department of the council in 1893.

Public transport

In 1877, the Imperial Tramways Company applied for a licence to run a tramway in the borough. The council saw this as an opportunity to get the company to pay part of the cost of maintaining the roads along which the tramways ran, and so they agreed to the proposal. The initial horse-drawn service ran from Cemetery Junction to Brock Barracks on Oxford Road, and by 1880 it was carrying 12,000 people per week. It operated on a 4ft gauge track, narrower than many tramways. The council had an option to buy out the private company, which it exercised in 1901, at a cost of £11,394. It immediately brought forward plans to replace the horse-drawn trams by electric ones, which came into operation in July 1903. It also introduced improved working conditions for the drivers and their horses. Driver's wages were raised by 6d. to 4s. a day for a seventy hour week, with one day

A horse-drawn tram on Oxford Road, near Reading West Bridge, in about 1900.

Reading fire brigade in about 1900.

off in nine. The horses' rations were increased to 20lb of corn a day. The electric trams which replaced the horses ran until May 1939, when they were replaced by trolley buses and motor buses.

The old tramways depot building at Mill Lane survives as a reminder of this era and there are plans to incorporate it as part of the Oracle development.

Water and Drains – the Birth of the Whitley Whiff!

Early nineteenth-century Reading was not the place to live if you wanted a long and healthy life. The life expectancy of a resident of Reading at that time was five years less than for someone who lived in Wokingham. Death rates were between 50 and 100 per cent higher than the national average, just about the highest in Britain.

The reasons were not difficult to find. A report into the sanitary conditions of the town was commissioned in 1846. The results showed that 95 per cent of the borough had no proper drainage of any kind. All their foul water ran into cesspools, which in turn found their way into the water courses. The Royal Commission on the Health of Towns found Reading to be 'nothing but an extended cesspool'. Of the 4,155 houses in the borough, almost 2,000 had no water supply at all, while 390 drew their water direct from the Kennet. Over three times that number used the Kennet as their sewer and a variety of industries discharged their noxious waste products into the river.

This problem was not a new one. As long ago as 1576 the Commission for Sewers laid down stringent rules against contaminating the water supplies, which were universally ignored. In 1595 the complaint was made that the water and filth in Butcher Row on Broad Street 'standeth in such sort that in winter time people cannot well pass'. Attempts to solve some of these problems also had a long history. The Reading Water Company was originally set up in 1696, with a covenant to supply water to the borough for a thousand years. Their waterworks at Mill Lane proved totally unequal to the task and quickly fell into disuse. The company was revived again in 1802, but its efforts seem to have been little more successful.

A description of the water supply system in operation in 1814 makes one wonder how any Reading resident survived at all. Water was pumped from the Kennet, along wooden pipes which were no more than bored-out elm trees, into a lead reservoir which stood in the centre of Broad Street. The water was totally untreated and dark chocolate brown in colour. Any fish or eels that were able to survive in the Kennet tended to get sucked up the pipes and caused blockages until they decomposed. Water was only pumped on alternate days. In the 1820s, a water tower was erected to supply some of the higher houses and a more powerful pump was fitted, but the lack of any form of purification continued.

The attitude of some prominent local people had much to do with this state of affairs. As late as 1859, Alderman Brown was able to argue that the prevention of fever was 'impious' and that to suggest a good drainage system would prevent disease 'was saying more than mortal man ought to do'. *The Times* similarly argued against people being 'bullied into health'. A strong lobby of 'economizers' existed on the council, whose objections to improved drainage probably had more to do with the effects on the borough's rates than any ethical consideration.

The public health reform movement gathered force across Britain in the 1840s, but the economizers fought against it in Reading. In 1858, the borough surveyor, John Marshall, presented proposals for providing the town with mains drainage. The economizers on the council opposed them. Four years earlier, cholera had broken out in the town, but there were still those who denied the link between dirt and disease (or man's right to do anything about it). The plan had only been drawn up at all because Lord Palmerston, who was then the home secretary, had recommended to the Local Board of Health that the works be completed without delay. Marshall's modest scheme was costed at £9,000, a capital sum that would have required a 2d. rate over thirty years. It became an issue in the municipal elections of 1858 and the scheme was eventually abandoned.

The council's opposition to any kind of improvement continued into the 1860s. In 1866 it lobbied against the Thames Navigation Bill, aimed at preventing local authorities from discharging sewage into the Thames and its tributaries. Only in 1867 did it finally decide to acquire land outside the borough to establish a sewage farm. Seven hundred and sixty acres of land at Whitley, including Manor Farm, were acquired by compulsory purchase order at a cost of £102,000. The cost of the works associated with the scheme was £228,000. A special Act of Parliament was obtained in 1870 to give the council the neces-

Blake's Lock pumping station and the sluices. This photograph can be dated exactly – Saturday, 9 June 1900.

sary powers. The main sewers and the pumping house at Blake's Lock were completed in 1875 and the first house was connected to the system in November of that year. By 1880, six thousand out of a planned eight thousand houses were connected to the sewers.

From Blake's Lock, the sewage was pumped through pipes along the bed of the River Kennet to Manor Farm. There, the sewage was simply spread on the farmland and left for nature to break it down. Once this was done, the land was once again farmed. The soil was evidently so fertile that mangels grown there carried off first prize in both local and national agricultural shows! The farm itself was making a gross profit of over £1,200 by 1877/8, but the rest of the sewerage scheme proved to be a major burden on local finances for years to come. By 1879, almost half the rates went on debt payments for the loans on the sewerage scheme.

Meanwhile, improvements to the supply of fresh water were still needed. As late as 1874, water shortages led to the water supply being turned off each night. But in December of that year a fire broke out at the Great Western Railway works. Without water to fight it, the fire raged out of control, causing serious damage. This led to the construction of a new reservoir at Bath Road, but its efficiency was reduced by a series of broken mains in the 1880s. Even after the borough was extended, the council was still struggling to provide a pure and reliable source of water. The water was pumped to the reservoir from Southcote pumping station. This was near Fobney Lock and upstream of where most of the pollution of Reading poured into the Kennet. This was opened in 1850 and was only replaced by the new waterworks nearby in 1982.

One further advance for public health in the nineteenth century was the creation of an adequate cemetery. By the early nineteenth century, the town's churchyards were filled to over-flowing. Eye-witnesses at the time told of grave-diggers hacking up partly decomposed corpses, to make room for the next occupant of the grave. The problem was solved in 1843 when a private company, the Reading Cemetery Company, opened a new cemetery just outside the then borough boundary. The new cemetery gave its name to Cemetery Junction and the company remained in private hands until the council took it over in 1887. There was strict segregation in the cemetery, between 'church' (which got 6 of the 10 acres) and 'chapel', which got the rest. The Cemetery Gateway, which forms a major landmark in this part of the town, was restored by the council in recent years.

Journeys

The pictures on the followng pages show the people of Reading travelling around the town or away from it. Some are just going about their everyday business; others are celebrating the dawn of a new era of transport in Reading; and the men at Reading station are about to experience a dramatic change in their lives.

Caversham Road, from the railway bridge, during the floods of 1894.

Broad Street. The people of Reading celebrate the opening of the electric tram service in 1903.

Cheerful volunteers for the 35th Division, Signals Company, leave Reading station for training at Ripon, 16 July 1915. By January 1916, they would be seeing action in the trenches in France, including the Battles of the Somme and Passchendaele.

The Reading-to-Tilehurst Omnibus and its proprietor, Mr A. Ilsley, pictured in about 1900.

Reading the Shopping Centre – Broad Street

Reading today is one of the most important shopping centres in the south-east and Broad Street is its heart. For most of Reading's history, however, this was not the case. Broad Street as a major shopping street was very much a nineteenth and twentieth-century creation.

THE STREET MARKET

In the earliest days of the town, shopping would have centred around St Mary's Butts and the church. It was the growth of the Abbey that shifted the centre of the town to the east and led to the creation of the street market in Market Place. For several centuries the street market remained there. It was only in 1973 that it moved back to its present location in Hosier Street.

The market would have supplied many of the needs of local people. It was as big as the present street market by the early nineteenth century, opening on Wednesday for meat, vegetables and fruit and on Saturdays for corn. The town was packed on market days and a great deal of business was done. In the second half of 1842, for example, traders took receipts of over £90,000.

Around 1800 a new market hall was built just off Market Place, for traders selling foodstuffs. One visitor to the market hall around that time complained that the traders used to obstruct the way through with their goods. Freshly slaughtered animals used to overhang the pavement, dripping blood on to unfortunate passers-by!

At this time, corn was still sold in the open in Market Place itself. It was not until 1854 that a new corn exchange was built to the west of Market Place, on the site occupied today by the Market Arcade. The main entrance to the corn exchange was a

106

grand 'triumphal arch' on Broad Street. This has gone today, but the side entrance from Market Place is still there, built in a mock Renaissance style.

STREET VENDORS

Street vendors have long been part of the retail life of the town. Early nineteenth-century accounts tell of cakes, milk and fish all being sold door to door. The cake vendor also had the job of pumping the organ at his local church. On one famous occasion, he fell asleep in church and, dreaming that he was at his weekday job, began bellowing 'Nice, new cakes! Here they be! Two sizes bigger than last week!' in the middle of the service!

Before that, during the seventeenth century, one Vincent Lancellus, 'Arrabian by nation and a doctor of fisicke', was practising his variety of medicine in the streets of Reading under the licence of the Archbishop of Canterbury.

More recently, the town has had everything from banana salesmen touring the streets, to a man selling 'Grandma's Chest Tablets' from a barrow next to the Vaudeville Cinema in Broad Street.

BROAD STREET

Although most food shopping was done in Market Place, Broad Street was the site of Reading's sheep market during its heyday as a woollen town. Sheep pens lined the length of Broad Street on market days and farmers brought sheep there from many miles around.

As the earliest maps of Reading show, the eastern end of Broad Street was divided in two by a row of buildings, to form Fishe Strete and Buchers Row. The names give an indication of the trades carried on there, in conditions that would horrify the modern shopper. Animals were slaughtered in view of the public, and blood and offal ran out into the street. In the days before refrigeration the meat went off rapidly in the hot weather and had to be given away to the poor. In winter, pools of rainwater added to the other filth made the streets virtually impassable. It was only in 1862 that these properties were demolished.

107

Two views of Union Street. (*Above*) Mr W. H. Moore, cutler of Union Street, from around 1900. (*Below*) 'Smelly Alley' in 1945, complete with war-time queues.

Broad Street in 1870. The street still looks as if it belongs in a small market town. It was due to undergo a major transformation in the next thirty years.

Before the nineteenth century, Broad Street was much more mixed than it is today. It was partly residential (William Laud, the future Archbishop of Canterbury, was born there and William Simonds spent part of his early life there), there were coaching inns (the Angel stood on the site now occupied by British Home Stores), manufacturing (Simonds Brewery started its life there) and commercial activities (Simonds, again, opened his bank there in 1790); there was even religion, with the establishment of the United Reform Church there in 1662.

HEELAS

During the nineteenth century, retailing began to predominate and some of the names we see in Broad Street today began to appear. John Heelas opened a small drapery shop in Minster Street in 1854. His sons, John and Daniel, joined him in the business, which soon diversified into carpets, furniture and funerals (until well into this century, Heelas had a monumental masonry department). The shop expanded, buying in neighbouring premises. By 1929 they had bought up the Black Boy public house and had established a presence on Broad Street.

A somewhat retouched photograph of Heelas's premises in Minster Street in 1875.

Heelas soon developed a reputation for quality. Queen Mary used to shop there and one writer remembers as a small boy being intimidated by a stern one-armed commissionaire in a grey uniform, who used to patrol outside. Among their more unusual customers were Reading gaol, to whom they supplied prison uniforms (mens' 17s. 10d., boys' 13s. 9d.). One customer they would prefer to forget is Victorian murderess Annie Dyer: Heelas supplied the white tape with which she strangled her infant charges.

The family interest in Heelas was bought out by millionaire Charles Clore in 1947, became part of the United Drapery Stores Group in 1950 and finally joined the John Lewis Partnership in 1953.

MCILROYS

A rival to Heelas opened to the north side of Oxford Road in 1903. William McIlroy's store, known locally as 'Mac's', was one of the architectural wonders of the town. It had huge windows at ground and first-floor levels and elaborately decorated terracotta on its upper storeys. The building became known as Reading's Crystal Palace and survives to this day, opposite Broad Street Mall. Part of the upper storeys provided living accommodation for the staff.

MARKS AND SPENCER

Marks and Spencer opened their first lock-up shop in West Street in 1904. The sign above the door read 'Marks and Spencer. Originators of Penny Bazaars. Admission Free'. The front was indeed completely open, like a bazaar. They opened up a second store in Broad Street in 1912, where they gradually expanded their activities. The West Street store closed in 1936.

MILWARDS

In the nineteenth century, most high street shops were still in family ownership. Milwards is one which remains so. It was founded in a tiny cottage in Basingstoke in 1857. They opened a branch in Reading in 1890, and in 1902 made Reading their headquarters and warehouse. They now have a new building on the site in Church Street, to which they originally moved in 1913.

As the twentieth century advanced, more of the familiar high street names appeared. Woolworths came to Reading in 1923. Shortly after modernizing the store in 1932, it suffered a disastrous fire. Reading Cooperative Society, which had existed since 1860, built their new store on Cheapside in 1928.

One thing that Broad Street lacked until the very end of the nineteenth century was a direct link to the station. This was remedied by Charles Fidler, local businessman and member of the council. He promoted the construction of Queen Victoria Street, whose yellow brick and terracotta buildings survive little changed to this day. Unfortunately, he did not live to see his brainchild finished, since he died in 1903 as it was nearing completion.

The Borough Spreads Its Boundaries
– Caversham and Tilehurst

Apart from the Thames, Reading has no natural features to contain its growth. For the past hundred years or more, the town has spread out beyond the borough boundaries and the boundaries have been a source of dispute with Reading's neighbours.

THE 1887 EXTENSION

In the 1880s, Reading borough was only about one-fifth of its present size. The urban fringe was growing rapidly, especially to the east, where it adjoined the area known as Earley. New Town

Caversham, seen from the Great Western railway station in about 1840.

was built, from the 1850s on, partly to house the growing workforce at Huntley and Palmers. The sewers from these houses were not connected to the borough's sewerage system, but discharged directly into the Kennet.

This was a great concern to the health authorities who, in 1876, asked that Earley's sewers be connected to the borough's system. The borough council at that time had not laid out enough land at Manor Farm to deal with the borough's own sewage, and decided not to agree to this proposal. Some of the council thought this should only happen if the borough's boundaries were extended into Earley, Whitley and Southcote.

The health authorities continued to lobby for the connection to be made. In 1884, the case began to be prepared for an extension of the borough boundary. There was disagreement between those who just wanted to take in the built-up area on the fringes, and those who looked wider, to take in areas likely to be developed in the future. There was even one member of the council already lobbying to take in Caversham.

Caversham Court and St Peter's church, in about 1890.

The *Berkshire Chronicle* in 1886 spoke of the council having an 'earth hunger'. 'What Bulgaria is to Russia, Earley is to Reading', they declared. In November of that year, a public meeting was held to discuss the council's extension plans. The meeting was well attended and largely hostile to the proposals. A poll of ratepayers was organized for 20 December and, thanks to some energetic lobbying by the council, a small majority in favour was obtained. The approval of Parliament was granted in the following year and Reading was more than doubled in size.

THE 1911 EXTENSION

By the twentieth century, Caversham had become less of a village than a residential suburb of Reading. Tilehurst was also expanding beyond the borough boundary. In 1908, the borough council began moves to take these areas into Reading.

In Tilehurst, drainage was once again an important part of the case. The borough council proposed including the area in its mains drainage, and now had the capacity to do so. They were also opposed to Bradfield Rural District Council's proposal to

St Michael's church, Tilehurst, in about 1790.

Pleasure boats and a hire launch at the Roebuck in Tilehurst, in about 1890.

build a separate sewage works at Scours Lane. This would have prejudiced the Thames Side Promenade, which the council had laid out as a recreational area in 1907. In this area, the proposal was generally supported by the public and the local authorities. The borough council had also carried out some major capital investment in this part of Tilehurst. Since 1887, they had bought Prospect Park, built the Park Fever Hosptial and enlarged the waterworks.

The case in Caversham was rather different. It relied on the argument that there was a community of interest between Caversham and Reading. People in Caversham had been lobbying for a new bridge across the Thames since 1899 and the likelihood of this being achieved would be much greater if both sides of the Thames were under the same local authority. A similar situation exists today with the long-awaited third Thames river crossing.

There was much more opposition to the incorporation of Caversham. The case of poaching land from another county, was, in any case, going to be more difficult to argue. However, many of

Caversham's services already came from south of the river and almost half of its population worked in Reading. Many of Caversham's other services were administered from Oxford, so that the case for running them more locally was strong. Reading was also able to demonstrate that the standard of many of Caversham's services was unsatisfactory.

Permission for the extension was granted in 1911, on condition that the borough council built a new bridge at Lower Caversham within five years. (As we saw earlier, its completion actually took much longer than that.)

Further proposals to expand the borough were advanced in 1947 and 1965, to reflect the continuing growth of the built-up area. Neither was successful. Today, the built-up area of Greater Reading has a population of over two hundred thousand, only one hundred and thirty thousand of whom live within the borough. The debate about the town's boundaries looks set to continue into the future.

The Story of Reading in Maps

Maps are a wonderful medium for understanding the growth and change of settlements. They enable the reader to get behind the surface of a place in a way that is not possible with photographs or drawings.

The maps on the following pages show more than three hundred years in the development of Reading, from the earliest surviving map to views of Reading within living memory. They are taken from collections held by Reading Museum and Art Gallery, Reading Central Library and the Planning Department of Reading Borough Council. In the sequence that follows each map page is preceded by a descriptive account.

MAP OF REDDING, 1611, BY JOHN SPEED

This is the earliest surviving map of Reading, and already many of the features of the modern town centre can be seen. At the top right is the Abbey, already partly in ruins. Sir Francis Knollys, six-times MP for Reading, lived in the Abbeye House. Close to 'the Greate Gate into the Forbury' were gardens from where the local children stole flowers and sold them.

The Market Place nearby has an extra row of houses built into it. Around the same time this map was drawn, John Blagrave left £200 to the town, to demolish them and enlarge Market Place. It was at the same time that he provided the money to build the Blagrave Piazza on to the south side of St Laurence's church. In the middle of Market Place stood 'the Plumpe' and well, leased by the corporation for 4d. a year. Nearby were the whipping post, pillory, ducking stool (an early punishment for scolds – women given to using abusive language) and the stocks.

Greyfriars Priory is shown at top left. Enough of the Greyfriars buildings remained intact for them to be a suitable lodging for the wife of King James I, when she visited Reading. Minster Street was at this time very narrow and blocked by wagons. The problem became so bad' that the corporation closed it off with chains in the vicinity of Chain Street, giving the street its name.

The area on which Simonds Brewery was later to be built at this time consisted of a series of islands. Five bridges can be seen between St Mary's Butts and the present-day line of the Inner Distribution Road. Seven Bridges House, built by Simonds on this site, still stands today. (It is not clear from this map which two other bridges make up the seven in the name – possibly the two over the Holy Brook, to the east of Bridge Street?) The Bear Inn stood on Bridge Street and dated back to 1483. It gives its name to Bear Wharf. Cromwell visited it in 1648, receiving gifts from the corporation there, and Coleridge wrote *Religious Musings* in its tap room.

The mill, from which Mill Lane takes its name, can be seen. A mill had stood there since the days of the Domesday Book and was to survive into the early days of the twentieth century. Ort

Lane is now known as Watlington Street. Some of the streets shown here had even earlier names. Hosier Street was previously known as Lormery Lane (where lorimers manufactured horses' bits). Cross Street is shown on this map as Gutter Lane, a name dating back at least to 1272.

REDDIN

A	The Priorye
B	Gutter lane
C	The Free Schole
D	St Laurence
E	Forbery
G	Queens stables
H	The Abbey
K	Schomakers Row
L	Fishe strete
M	Buchers Rowe
N	Brode stret
P	Pangburne lane
Q	Hosier lane
R	Castell Strete
S	S. Maryes
T	Minster strete
V	Chayne lane
W	George lane
X	London strete
Z	Mill Lane
3	Seaven Bridges
4	S Giles church
5	Towne Mills
6	High Bridge
7	S. Giles strete
8	Crowne lane

9	Ort lane
10	Swier stret
11	Old Streate
12	Dukes stret

Coly

Speed's map of Reading, 1611

READING AND THE SURROUNDING AREA
– THOMAS PRIDE, 1790

Almost two hundred years have passed since Speed drew his map, but the shape of the town looks little changed. The first population census would not be held for another eleven years, but the population of Reading by 1801 was still less than 10,000.

Many of Reading's stately homes were already in evidence. Calcot Park House and the house on Prospect Hill, which formed the basis of the Mansion House, were both built in the 1750s. At Maiden Erleigh, the old house was to be greatly enlarged during the late nineteenth century by millionaire Solomon Barnato Joel. He gave his name to the Sol Joel Playing Fields, which were opened by the Duke of York (later King George VI) in 1927. The house was demolished in 1960.

Earley Court was formerly the manor house of Erleigh St Bartholomew. The house was built between the sixteenth and eighteenth centuries and was once the home of Lord Sidmouth. It was demolished in 1935.

Coley House was, from around 1309, the property of the Vachell family. Charles I was entertained there during the Civil War. The original house was demolished some time during the eighteenth century, though the dovecote (dating from 1593) and farm buildings on the site of the house survive. Just after this map was drawn, the house passed out of the ownership of the Vachell family. A new house was built on higher ground. This was later occupied by the Monck family, who were leading lights in the life of the town throughout the nineteenth century. The new house still stands and has recently been refurbished.

Many of the names on the map are familiar, but the spellings differ from their modern counterparts. For example, the map shows Tylehurst, Emmir Green, King's Mead, Chase Farm, Shinefield, Henly, Sunning, Bullmarsh and Kidmoor End. One explanation of this may be illiteracy on the part of the map makers or the people who gave them information.

Red Lane is an ancient highway, known as Rudden Lane by the

Saxons. The land on which it was built was once part of the Abbey lands. It was part of an endowment made to the local leper hospital by the Abbot of Reading in 1160.

The New Inn was later to become the Marquis of Granby. Earlier still, it was known as the Gallows Tavern. It was the last stop on the route from Reading Gaol to the gallows at Earley. New Farm was later to become the site of New Town.

Bullmarsh Heath was the site of Reading's race course up until the early part of the nineteenth century. The heath was enclosed in about 1816. When this happened, local people lost the right to cut heather as fuel on the heath, as well as their horseracing.

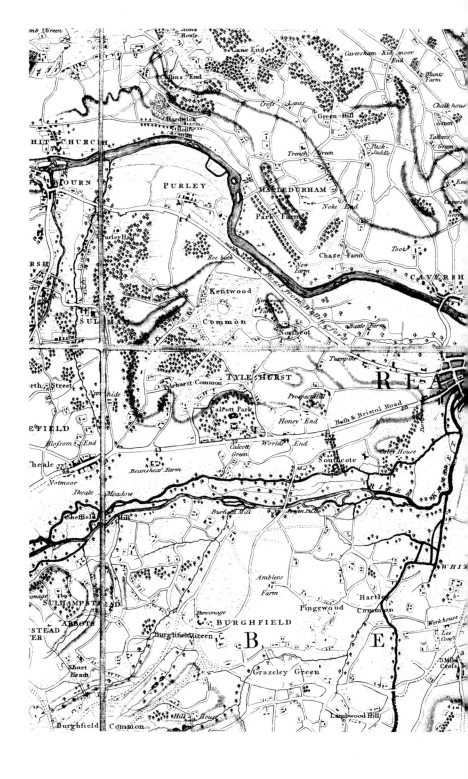

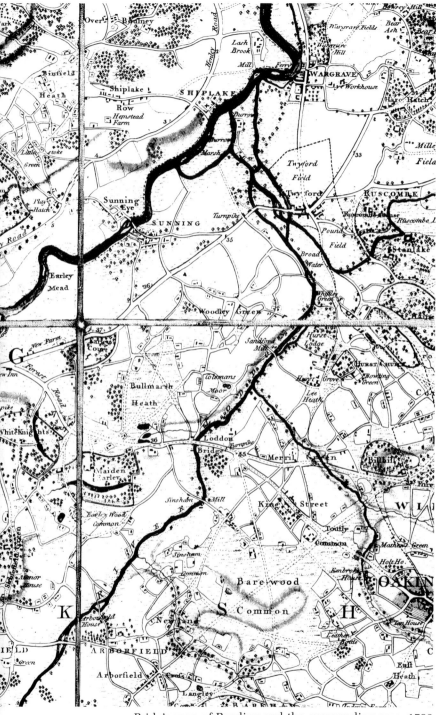

Pride's map of Reading and the surrounding area, 1790

READING TOWN CENTRE, 1871

When Brunel built his first station building in 1840, very little of the area to the north of the railway was built up. The same is true over thirty years later. What is perhaps more surprising is that the area immediately opposite the station is still undeveloped. It was to remain so until the 1960s, when the present shops and the Western Tower office block were built. The map shows clearly how all the land around the station was raised on embankments, lifting it out of the floodplain.

The area around Valpy Street also has yet to be built upon. Valpy Street itself has only recently been created (so recently that it does not yet bear its name on the map). The site of the future museum and art gallery is occupied by the county court office. Many other streets which are part of the town centre today have not yet made their appearance. Queen Victoria Street would not be built for another thirty years. Reading Bridge and the road leading up to it was fifty years away. Sackville Street, near Greyfriars church, is not yet built and Garrard Street does not link through to Station Road.

The Great Western Railway still has separate 'up' and 'down' stations, with a third terminus for the South-Eastern Railway. The original terminus for the SER was a single, small platform on the north side of Forbury Road. It was only moved to its location near the GWR station around 1860.

One of the striking things the map shows is the number of back gardens that still survive in the heart of the town centre.

Historically, Reading has never been short of pubs. The maps shows no less than eleven pubs, inns, taverns and hotels on Broad Street alone. Nor has the age of the smaller brewer yet passed. One can be seen on Caversham Road and there are malthouses on Tudor Road, Merchants Place and near what is today the site of the Harris Arcade.

At the bottom of the map, St Mary's Butts still has almshouses fronting on to the churchyard and cottages in its centre. The northern end of the Butts is still very narrow. It was widened to ease the movement of traffic in the 1930s.

The veterinary infirmary shown on Friar Street was a hospital for sick and lame horses. Some of the worst-treated horses in the town were said to be those that pulled the horse buses and trams. This seems to be borne out by some of the photographs which exist of the unfortunate creatures.

The Athenaeum, at 146 Friar Street, started life as a library and philosophical institution. It was converted into a men's club in 1841 and flourished until long after the Second World War.

The Green School, which can be seen on the north side of Broad Street, was a boarding school founded in St Mary's Butts in 1782. It moved to the site on Broad Street in 1790 and was to remain there for almost a century. It was a charitable institution, whose purpose was to train up young girls to become domestic servants or apprentices. It took its name from the colour of the dresses worn by the pupils.

Reading Town Centre, 1871

EMMER GREEN, 1898

The Emmer Green shown on the map is a tiny settlement in the middle of open countryside. It will not become part of Reading until 1911. Buckingham Drive does not yet exist and the road to town is the winding Old Peppard Road, the route used by King Charles I in his retreat from the Battle of Caversham Bridge. There are several ponds, in addition to the one we know today. One is on the line of Buckingham Drive and another next to Park Farm, where the shopping precinct now stands. They may all once have been part of a much larger lake. The stream leading southwards from the pond is thought to be the one known as The Swillies, which finds its way down to the Thames. It originally formed the boundary to the Caversham Park Estate.

The post office is across the road from its present site, which has been occupied by a blacksmith since the sixteenth century. Hodges Post Office Stores provided for some of the shopping needs of the villagers, and groceries were also for sale at the White Horse Inn until the 1920s. In the yard at the back of the Black Horse Inn is the headquarters of the local fire brigade.

Many of the local people may have worked at the brick works at the junction of Kiln Road and Peppard Road, just off the top of the map, and its products may have been used to build the village houses. The brick kiln in Emmer Green was built around 1654 on land known as Hamer's Field. The village school was built in 1876, replacing one that was opened in 1866. This one in turn was to close in 1933, due to lack of support. Only large-scale building in the area after the Second World War would create the demand for modern primary schools at The Hill, Peppard Road (1950) and Grove Road. The recreation ground was in those days an open village green. In 1902 the villagers built a huge bonfire there to celebrate the coronation of Edward VII. Two men slept inside it the night before to guard it from arsonists.

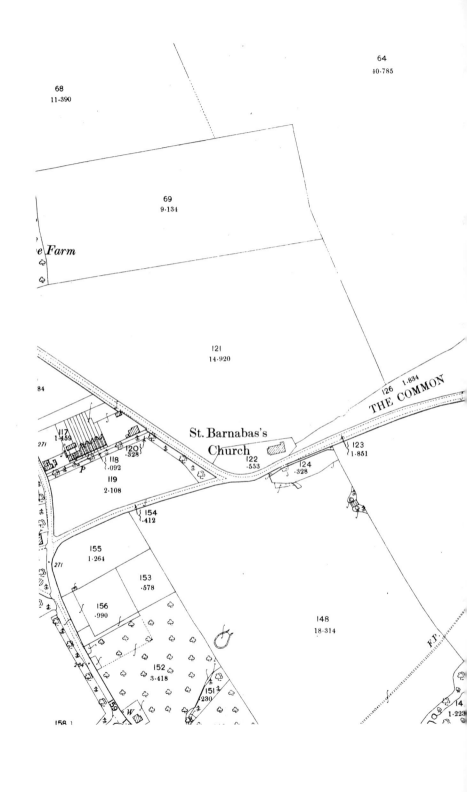

64
40·785

68
11·390

69
9·134

e Farm

121
14·920

126 1·834

THE COMMON

84

117
1·459

271

120
·328

118
·092

119
2·108

St. Barnabas's
Church

122
·553

123
1·851

124
·328

154
·412

155
1·264

271

153
·578

156
·990

148
18·314

F P

152
3·418

151
·230

14
1·223

159

W

158

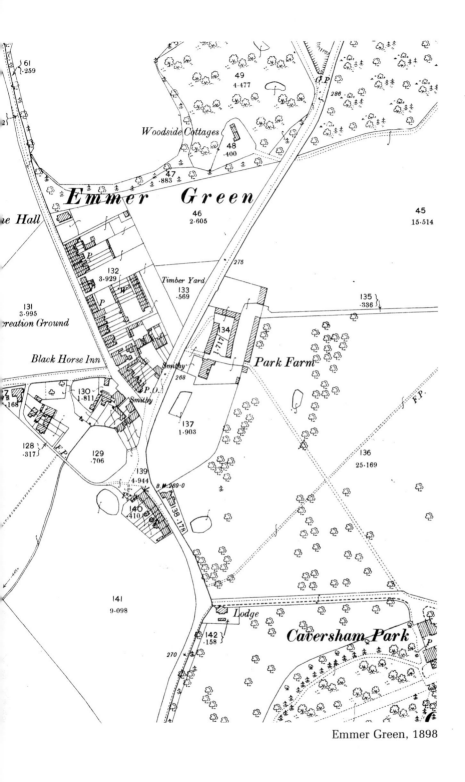

Emmer Green, 1898

SURLEY ROW, 1898

Surley Row, now one of the town's conservation areas, is one of the oldest parts of Caversham. It is crossed by a footpath, following the line of modern-day Rotherfield Way. It was down this footpath that pall bearers would carry former residents of Emmer Green, for burial in St Peter's churchyard. Pall bearing being thirsty work, they would normally stop at the Gardener's Arms beer house, no doubt leaving the deceased propped up in some suitable corner. The Gardener's Arms is still a public house, though the building that occupies the site is a more recent one.

One of the oldest buildings in the area is Tudor Cottage, which stands at the junction of Surley Row and Rotherfield Way. Built in the sixteenth or seventeenth century, the garden wall was added in the eighteenth century and the building was recently extended, in keeping with the existing structure.

Grove Cottage, next door, is a more recent addition, being built in the 1830s in what was known as Tudor Gothic style. It was described in 1843 as 'a neat red brick building in the Elizabethan style'.

Caversham Grove, now part of the Highdown School buildings, dates originally from the early eighteenth century. It was altered and extended around 1878–80 by the eminent Victorian architect, Richard Norman Shaw. He was one of the early champions of the original Queen Anne style of the house. Although he almost doubled its size, much of his detailing is faithful to the original house.

The house was built, probably on the site of an earlier building, by Henry Smith, who became high sheriff of Oxfordshire in 1731. There is a memorial to his first wife in St Peter's churchyard. Another high sheriff – David Fell – lived there in later years. He died in 1806 and one of the woods on the estate was named after him. It was bought in 1878 by Frederick Saunders, the chairman of the Great Western Railway, who commissioned the extensions and who lived there for the next thirty years. In addition to the house, a barn (now used as a music room at the school) and a stable block survive from the late seventeenth or early eighteenth century.

A chalybeate spring was discovered in the grounds of Springfield House in 1803. This is a spring whose water contains iron, which is kept in solution by the presence of carbonic acid gas. The water apparently had a strong astringent taste when fresh from the spring but, exposed to the air, soon lost its freshness and smelt sulphurous.

Presumably working on the premises that anything tasting this bad must be doing you good, it became fashionable to drink these waters. This was despite the fact that some users suffered nausea, vomiting, stomach pains, heaviness of the head, vertigo and 'a sense of fullness over the whole body'. Miraculous cures were reported; the sight of one man was restored and everything from ulcers to rheumatism were cured by it. Bottles were sold in shops throughout the area.

Springfield was the home of Sir Rufane Donkin, a distinguished soldier, politician and man of letters. His unusual Christian name comes from a General Rufane, under whom his father served. He himself fought in the West Indies, Portugal and in India, where his wife Elizabeth died, leaving him with an infant son. Physically and mentally shattered by his loss, he was invalided to the Cape Province, where he later took on the job of caretaker governor. It was here that he named a newly-founded town Port Elizabeth, after his late wife. Donkin Hill is named after him (it was previously called The Slopes). The house itself was an early nineteenth-century villa. It later became the home of the convent of St Luke, and at the time of writing there are plans to convert it into flats.

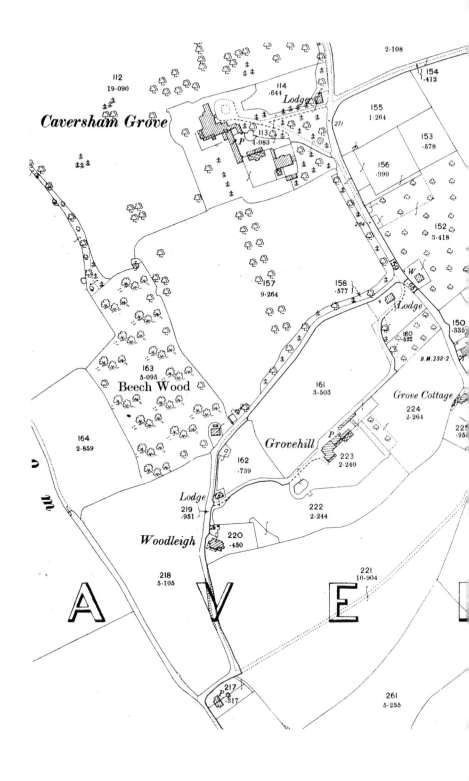

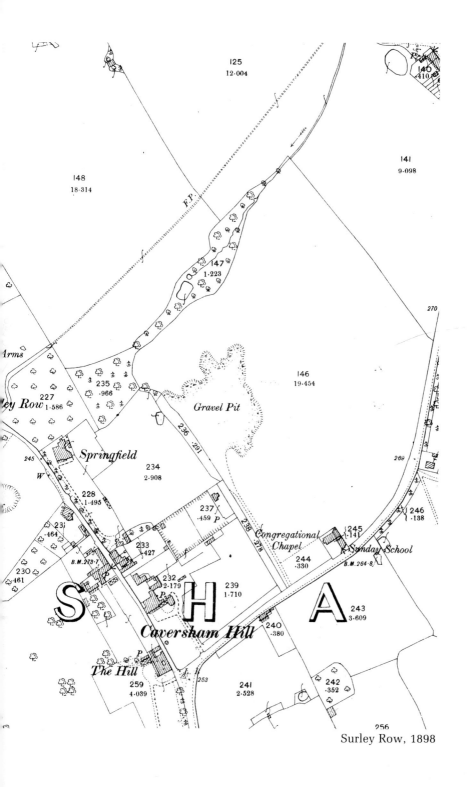

Surley Row, 1898

CAVERSHAM, 1899

Caversham was, at this time, a small freestanding settlement of less than ten thousand people on the north bank of the Thames. It was not yet part of Reading.

St Peter's church is one of the most ancient buildings shown on the map. It dates back to around 1100 and was built on land given by the Earl of Buckingham, the then lord of the manor of Caversham. The main doorway and the marble font of the present structure date back to Norman times. The church was badly damaged during the Civil War Battle of Caversham Bridge. It was restored in 1878/9 at a cost of £3,463 7s. 1d., at which time the present flint tower replaced an earlier timber structure. The churchyard contains monuments to the Crawshays, the family of nineteenth century ironmasters who owned Caversham Park, and the Freebody family, the long-established Caversham boat builders.

Next to the church stands Caversham Court, which was originally the rectory to St Peter's church. It was demolished in 1933, though the stable block and a gazebo remain. The grounds are now a public garden.

Somewhere in the vicinity of the church stood an important shrine to Our Lady. The first record of it is in 1199, but it is thought to have been in existence since at least the start of the twelfth century. The wooden statue of the madonna and child wore a gold and jewelled crown, and drew pilgrims from all over Britain. These included Catherine of Aragon, one of Henry VIII's wives. Shortly after her visit, the shrine was destroyed during the course of the dissolution of the monasteries.

The river near the bridge is described as the Buck Stream. This refers to the eel traps, or bucks, which stood there until 1911. The rights to these traps were held by the licensee of the Griffin, an ancient public house on Church Road. The public house shown on the map is not the present structure, which dates from 1906.

On the opposite side of the bridge stand a number of boat builders' premises. One of these is Willow Grotto, from where the Caversham family of Freebody ran their boat-building business. This was founded as long ago as 1257 and did not cease trading until 1964. The site now has flats on it.

Caversham Priory was demolished in 1967 to make way for the present shopping development. It is thought to have been built on the site of earlier houses, dating back at least to 1519. On the opposite side of Church Street to the priory can be seen an ancient right of way, known as the Cutting, leading down towards the river. Next to it is Caversham House, a Georgian stucco building demolished in 1966 to make way for St Martin's shopping precinct. Caversham House was once owned by Sir Rufane Donkin before he moved to Springfield House in Surley Row. About fifty years before this map was drawn up, the house came to be used as a school – Dr Knighton's Academy – which relocated there from Friar Street. It was linked to the playground on the opposite side of Church Street (where the library now stands) by a tunnel under the street. The Knighton family continued to occupy the house until at least the First World War, though the school closed somewhat earlier.

The junction of Hemdean Road and Church Street was the traditional site of the town's whipping post and possibly also the stocks, though these were later moved to Short Street.

On the west side of Prospect Street, set back slightly from the road and just to the south of Chester Street, stood a weaving shed. This survived until 1965, a relic of a former industry in Caversham, until it was demolished to make way for a shopping development.

The site of what is now the Prince of Wales pub car park was then occupied by thatched cottages. They were not to last long into the twentieth century. In 1907 they were burned down in a spectacular fire, watched by many of the residents of Caversham. Just on the edge of the map is St Anne's School, founded in 1894, but with origins going back to the seventeenth-century Grey Coat Hospital Charity School, founded in Westminster. Before that, the premises used to house a boys' school, called Amersham Hall.

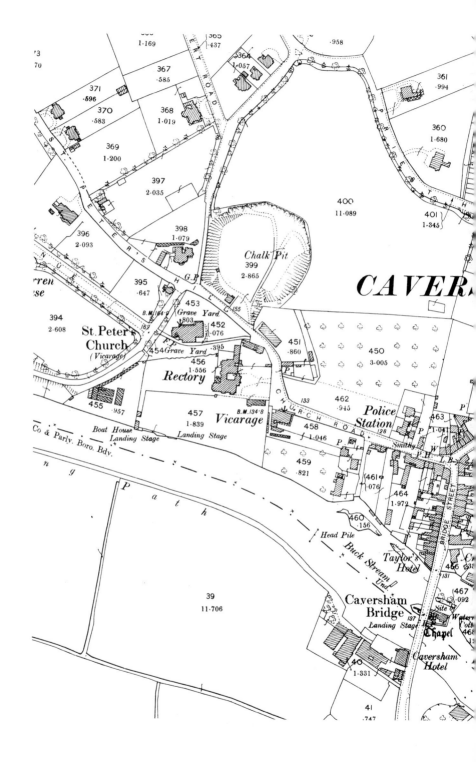

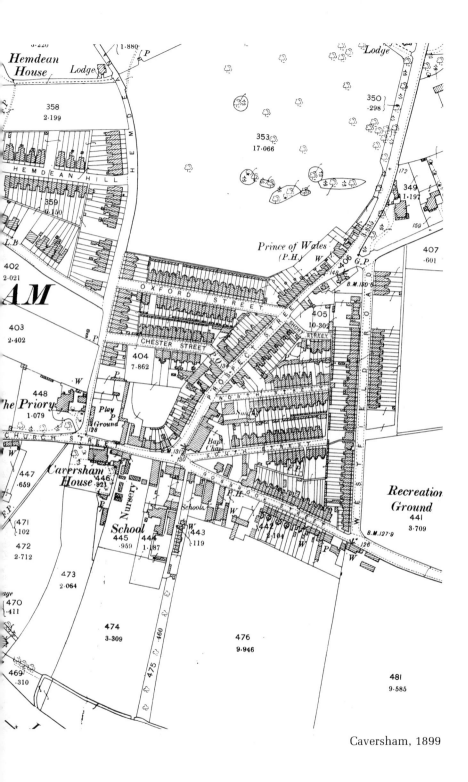

Caversham, 1899

WHITLEY HILL, 1899

Although the map is dated 1899, the borough boundary shown in the bottom left-hand corner of the map is the one that existed up until 1887. It was in that year that Reading expanded to take in the rest of Whitley and part of Tilehurst.

Whitley Hill has always played an important part in the life of Reading. According to some sources, the Abbey obtained its drinking water from a spring named the Conduit, near High-grove. It was said to possess medicinal qualities. A spring is shown on this map on Highgrove Street. Some historians also report that a private contractor agreed with the corporation to provide a supply of piped water from 'Cunditt Close' on Whitley Hill to Market Place. Whether this enterprise ever came to anything is difficult to know, since the town's first water company is generally held to have been set up in 1696, drawing water from the Kennet.

Conduit Close was also the site of the 'boarded houses', built and maintained by the corporation in the seventeenth century. These were the houses in which plague victims were isolated and left to their fate.

When civil engineer William Cubitt advised the corporation on the reconstruction of its water supplies in 1818, his proposals included a new reservoir at Spring Gardens, which can be seen at top left on the map. The area is now used as a playground.

As the population in this part of Reading grew, the congregation grew too large to fit into St Giles' church. Christchurch was planned to accommodate the overspill. It was completed in 1861/2 and enlarged in 1874. While they were waiting for it to be completed, the congregation used to meet in the school in Basingstoke Road (now St Paul's church hall). The architect of both the school and the church was Henry Woodyer. The vicarage, added in 1871, was designed by Alfred Waterhouse, of Town Hall fame. The 164ft spire of the church has been one of the town's landmarks for over a century.

The housing at the Mount was built by Huntley and Palmers in 1876 to house some of their growing army of clerical and managerial staff. The properties were carefully graded in accordance with the rank of the occupants. The mid-terraced properties were occupied by clerks, the end terraces by foremen, while the larger properties were for under-managers and managers. The Mount is now a conservation area.

Although some of the houses along Christchurch Road date back to around 1800, the area was largely rural in the early nineteenth century. A popular recreation at this time for Reading people was to walk up Doll's Walk – a track which led up Kendrick Hill roughly along the line of Kendrick Road – and from there across the open countryside to Whitley Wood.

In 1881, William Isaac Palmer rented some land off Christ's Hospital and built Hillside, the house on Allcroft Road which was later occupied by the Sutton family.

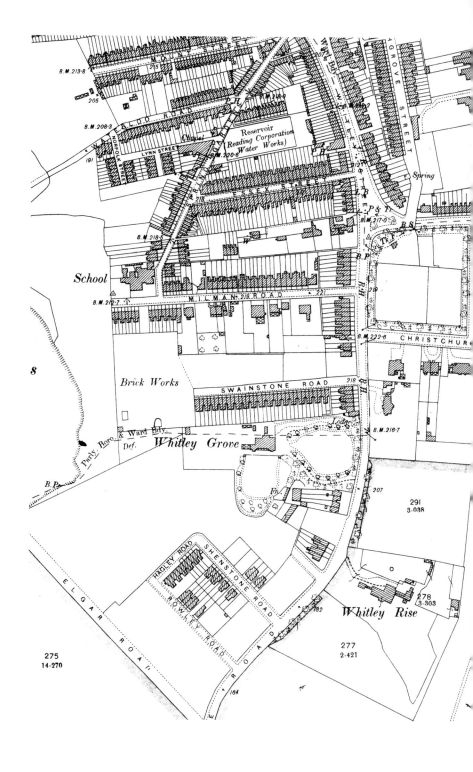

Whitley Hill, 1899

OXFORD ROAD AND BATTLE HOSPITAL, 1899

Battle Hospital was originally founded in 1867 as a workhouse to replace the three old parish institutions for the poor. It is shown on this map as the Reading Union Workhouse. Before 1834, people receiving poor relief in Reading were leading a good life. They were not required to do any work, were well fed and almost as well paid as labourers in work. Not surprisingly, few of its recipients wanted to come off poor relief.

The Poor Law Amendment Act of 1834 changed that. The old and the sick were still cared for, but the poorhouse of St Laurence's parish (at the west end of Friar Street) was turned into a workhouse. The inmates were kept to a strict regime of two meals a day, hard work, firm discipline and little contact with the outside world. The new buildings housed two hundred and fifty people – with the poor, the physically and mentally handicapped all in together, and a separate building for those with infectious diseases. In 1915, the armed forces took over the workhouse and it became Number One Reading War Hospital, caring for the wounded from the trenches in France. It was not until 1919 that the Poor Law system was replaced by the Local Government Act. The responsibilities of the Poor Law guardians were transferred to the local authorities and the workhouses became municipal hospitals.

The tramlines (they were horse-drawn trams at the time this map was drawn up) can be seen along Oxford Road, terminating at the Barracks. The Barracks were built in a special 'fireproof construction' by a Major Flint of the Royal Engineers in 1877. They were used, among other things, to house the militia on the occasion of their annual drills. Previously the militia had been housed in the hostelries of the town, which must have made it more difficult to maintain regimental discipline. The Barracks were, until 1959, the home of the Royal Berkshire Regiment. In that year, the Royal Berkshires were amalgamated with the Wiltshire Regiment to form the Duke of Edinburgh's Royal Regiment. The Barracks also have a miniature replica of the cenotaph in Whitehall, designed by Sir Edward Lutyens in 1921.

146

Elm Lodge, which now stands on Wilton Road, is an early nineteenth-century ashlar house (built in finely dressed stone). The map shows the carriage sweep in front of the house, which is now part of a housing association development.

A more modest landmark in the area, which appeared just after this map was drawn up, is the branch library. It was built in 1907 with funds provided by the philanthropist Andrew Carnegie. The ornate style of the building is known as 'Wren-aissance' and the busts on the front of the building are of Milton, Shakespeare and (it is thought) Darwin.

This stretch of Oxford Road was the scene of a notorious murder in 1817. A Roman Catholic priest, the Revd Father Longuet, was murdered for the money he was carrying. A reward of £250 was raised by public subscription for the arrest of the murderer. Rumour spread in the town was that the murderer was a member of a well-to-do local family and the suspect later attempted suicide in the River Kennet.

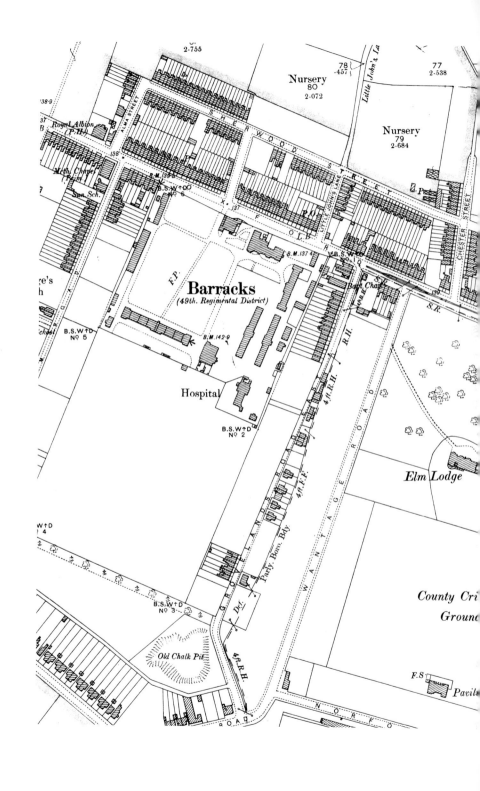

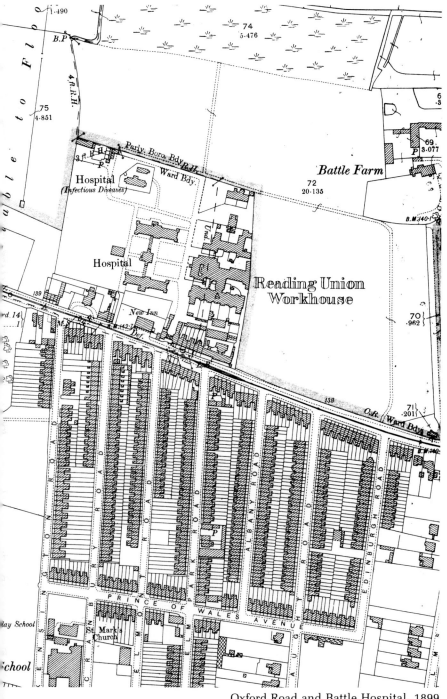

Oxford Road and Battle Hospital, 1899

HUNTLEY AND PALMERS, 1900

By the end of the nineteenth century, Huntley and Palmers were the biggest employers in Reading, with a workforce of over five thousand. The workforce had grown by more than tenfold since 1860, and the volume of biscuit production also grew apace – from 3,210 tons in 1860 to 16,562 tons in 1880. Transport was therefore an important part of the company's operations.

One of the factors which drew Huntley and Palmers to this site was the Kennet and Avon Canal. Since the 1830s, their biscuits had been distributed via the canal. Even after the coming of the railways they continued to use the canals. The more gentle movement of the barges meant fewer broken biscuits. But it was the railways that carried the bulk of their production. This map shows their extensive range of private sidings, covering a large part of their 24-acre site. It was partly to accommodate Huntley and Palmers' traffic that the new sidings at Kings Meadow Road and Vastern Road were opened in 1896. Fifty goods trains a day were coming to Reading each day by that time.

The two new goods yards were linked across Vastern Road by means of a level crossing. The longest trains were moved between the sidings at 1 a.m. to avoid delays to traffic in Vastern Road. According to one former Huntley and Palmers' employee, there was supposed to be a policeman on duty to superintend these movements, but he rarely showed up. Huntley and Palmers' locomotives had to work inside the warehouses. Conventional steam locomotives were unsuitable for this purpose, because of the fumes and the danger of fire from sparks. Instead Huntley and Palmers' bought special locomotives which were filled with high pressure steam from a stationary boiler. Each filling took fifteen minutes and gave two hours' running time. The last pair of these locomotives were bought in 1932. One of them has been preserved on the West Somerset Railway.

Huntley and Palmers' link with the Western Region ended in 1965 and the Southern region yard closed in 1970, around the time manufacturing began to be phased out after almost 130 years. The yards themselves closed fairly soon afterwards – the one at Kings Meadow Road in 1969 and Vastern Road in 1987.

Also shown on this map are the extensive premises of Suttons Seeds, to the east of Market Place. The industrial heritage of the canal can still be seen from the saw mills, timber yards and wharves to the south-west of the prison (now occupied by office development). To the west of Abbey Street a mill bridges the Holy Brook. A mill had been located there since medieval times, serving the Abbey. An archway bridging the Holy Brook is all that remains of it in 1991.

Just off this map is the area of New Town, built largely to house Huntley and Palmers' employees. The relative lack of pubs in parts of this area is accounted for by the fact that Palmer was a Quaker and a teetotaller.

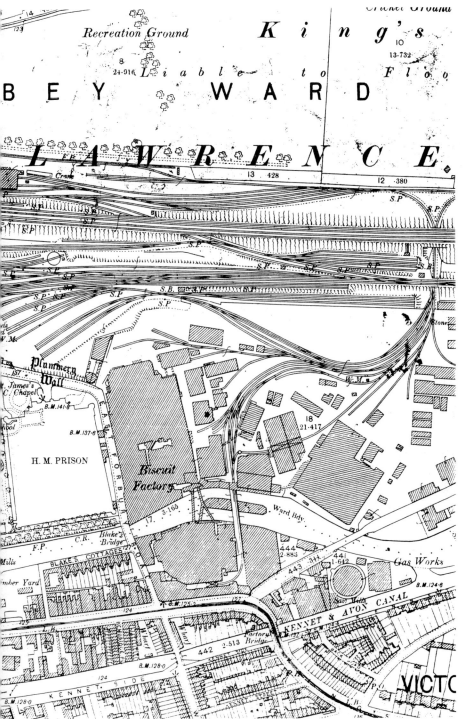

Huntley and Palmers, 1900

PROSPECT PARK AREA, 1911

The importance of the brick-making industry to this part of Reading is clear from this map. The Prospect Park brickworks occupies the site which now contains the Meadway shopping centre, and the area is covered with other brickworks, old and new. Only the old kiln near the junction of Honey End Lane and Meadway now survives.

Pegsgreen Lane, which follows the present line of Honey End Lane and Tilehurst Road, is an ancient highway described in 1840 as 'a track probably "as old as the hills" and retaining the rude simplicity and characteristic features of its early origin – winding, shady and here and there patches of greensward and the gipsy's glen and the glorious carol of the song thrush'. A far cry from the present Tilehurst Road in the rush hour!

It was along this track in 1688 that William of Orange and his Dutch troops passed on their way to London. On some old maps it originated on the Ridgeway, reaching Tilehurst via Hermitage, Bucklebury Common and Theale, entering Tilehurst via Pincents' Lane.

The map was drawn in 1911, the year in which the borough boundary was extended to take in Tilehurst. The boundaries shown here are the old ones, running up Water Road. It also marks the boundary of the Poor Law Union, the administrative area of the workhouse.

On the southern edge of the map is Honeyend Farm, which gives its name to Honeyend Lane.

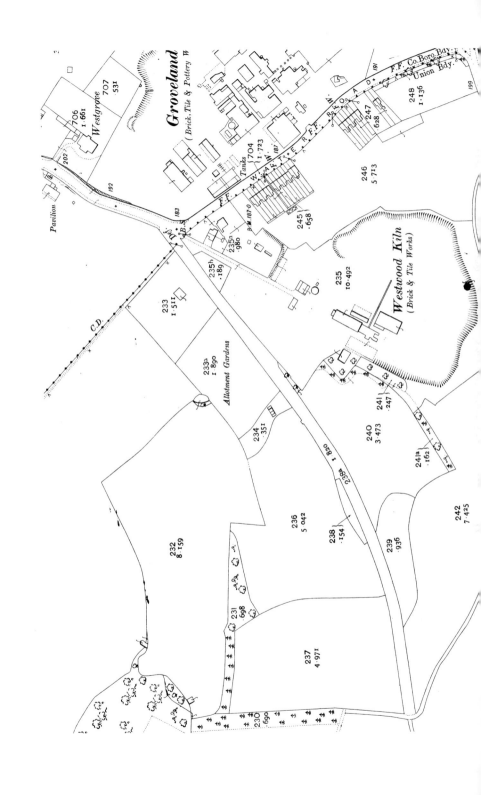

Groveland
(Brick, Tile & Pottery W

Westgrove
707
531

706
1·661

202

192

Pavilion
Def

183
B.M

Tanks
1704
1·723

B.M 187·0

F.F
W
T
A
E
R
F.F
W
F.F
W

245
·658

191

247
628

248
1·136

F.F. Co. Boro. Bdy.
Union Bdy.

199

246
5·713

235ᵃ
·980

235ᵇ
·189

233
1·511

235
10·492

Westwood Kiln
(Brick & Tile Works)

C.D.

233ᵃ
1·890

Allotment Gardens

234
351

241
247

240
3·473

241ᵃ
·162

238ᵃ

242
7·425

236
5·042

238
1·800

238
·154

239
·936

232
8·159

231
698

237
4·971

230
690

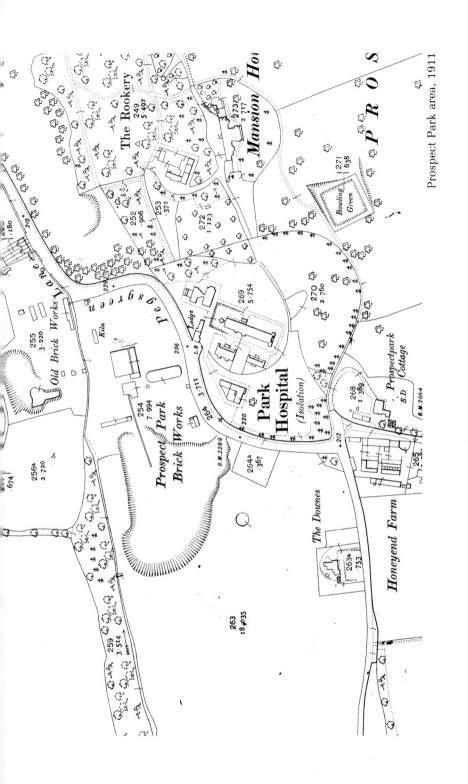

Prospect Park area, 1911

ST MARY'S BUTTS AND
THE SEVEN BRIDGES BREWERY, 1931

The map shows Simonds Brewery before its takeover by Courage in 1960 and its move to the new brewery next to the M4. The old brewery finally closed in 1980.

To the west of Bridge Street are À Larders Buildings, the almshouses originally funded by John Leche, who was known as John à Larder. His nickname came from his connection with the kitchens of the Abbey during the fifteenth century. The almshouses, originally given in 1476, were rebuilt between 1775 and 1790, and again in 1896. On the opposite side of Bridge Street, Gas Lane commemorates the establishment there in 1818 of the Reading Gas Light Company, who first brought gas street lighting to the town.

The brewery made extensive use of the canal to deliver its wares, but the railway was also an important form of transport. The rail links from the brewery into the Coley goods yard can be seen at the southern edge of the map. The Coley branch line was opened in 1908, largely to carry Simonds' products.

Bear Wharf takes its name from the Bear Inn, a hostelry dating back to 1483. It was in this Inn that the Law Courts were held in 1625, when they were driven out of London by the plague. The poet Coleridge hid from his creditors there. It originally stood on the corner of Castle Street, but later moved into Bridge Street. It was largely demolished around 1910.

The disappearance of the brewery is not the only thing that has brought dramatic change to this part of Reading. Since the Second World War, the construction of the Broad Street Mall, the civic centre and the Inner Distribution Road have all changed the character of the area to the west of St Mary's Butts.

Again, the map shows how industry congregated along the canal. Just south of County Lock is a tannery. In former years it would have been one of the many industrial processes discharging its noxious wastes into the canal. Much of the canal is also closed off to the public. Over a period of many years, the borough council has been successful in promoting the replacement of the industry with housing and leisure, and opening up the canal banks for public use.

To the west of London Street are the tin works of Huntley, Boorne and Stevens. Since the early nineteenth century, it had supplied Huntley and Palmers' with the tin boxes that were used to export their products all over the world. The works remained in London Street until the 1960s.

The People's Dispensary in Chain Street was established in 1802 to provide a rudimentary medical service for the people of Reading. By 1840 it came to occupy an imposing Bath stone building that stood on the east side of Chain Street until the 1980s, when the site was taken for part of the Heelas expansion.

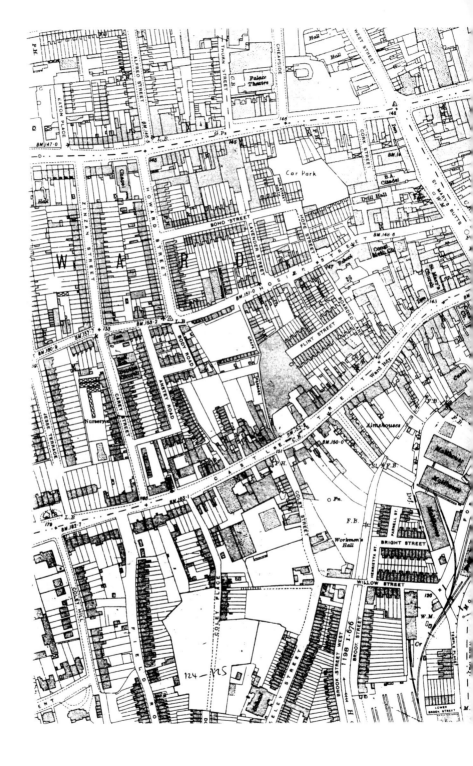

124—125

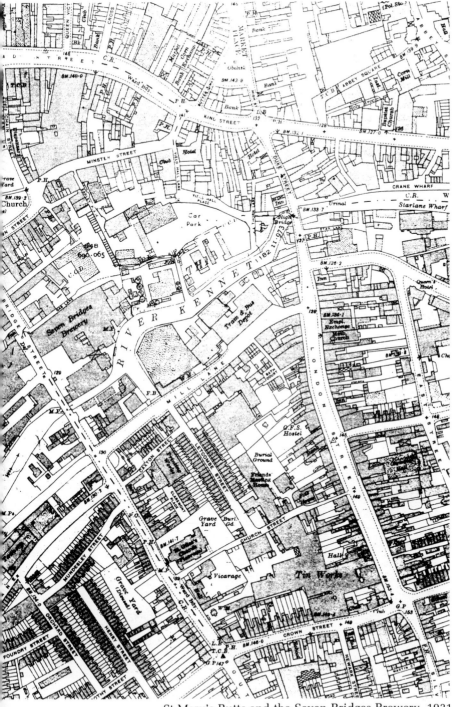

St Mary's Butts and the Seven Bridges Brewery, 1931

Some Reading People

This section looks at some of the people who were either born in Reading, or who made the town their home, and who won a national reputation for themselves.

WILLIAM LAUD, ARCHBISHOP OF CANTERBURY, 1573–1645

When he was a small child at school, the schoolmaster said to William Laud, 'When you are a little great man, remember Reading School.' Whether the teacher had an insight into Laud's future greatness we shall never know, but it is certainly true that

William Laud.

Laud maintained a close interest in the affairs of his home town throughout his life.

Laud was the son of a Reading clothier and grew up in a house which stood roughly where Queen Victoria Street now joins Broad Street. His father was active in the public life of the town, holding every office except mayor. Laud went to Reading School and then at sixteen became one of the first White scholars to go to St John's College, Oxford. (Sir Thomas White was another prominent native of Reading, who went on to become lord mayor of London and founder of St John's College. Reading was one of the schools he endowed with scholarships to the College.) Laud remained at the College until 1610, first as a student and, from 1589, as a fellow of the College. Seven months after leaving the College, he returned as its president.

In the years that followed, Laud made rapid progress through the church hierarchy. He was made King's chaplain in 1611, Prebendary of Lincoln (1614), Archdeacon of Huntingdon (1615), Prebendary of Westminster and Bishop of St David's (1621), Bishop of Bath and Wells, Dean of the Chapel Royal and a privy councillor (1626), Bishop of London (1628), Chancellor of Oxford University (1630) and finally Archbishop of Canterbury in 1633.

From his earliest days, Laud's high church, near-papist views and his fanatical hatred of puritanism made him enemies. As Archbishop of Canterbury, he was one of a triumvirate (with King Charles I and the Earl of Stafford) who tried to rule church and state with a rod of iron. However, the affairs of state did not prevent Laud from taking a close interest in events in Reading. His efforts to sort out the mismanagement of the Kendrick Charity are recorded elsewhere in this book (see p. 16). In 1634 he sent Sir Nathaniel Brent, the Vicar General, to conduct an inquiry into the spiritual health of the town. In 1636, he imposed his choice of schoolmaster on Reading School. Two years later, he obtained a charter for the town which was to be the basis for local government in Reading until 1835. In 1639 he got the right to nominate Reading's parliamentary representative. In the following year, he endowed the town with land worth £200 at Bray, which was used for various charitable purposes in Reading.

Laud's intolerance of Nonconformists was shown by the brutal treatment given to his opponents by the Court of Star Chamber. When a Reading man named Ludovic Bowyer spread rumours that Laud was under house arrest for treasonable dealings with the Pope, he was fined the enormous sum of £3,000, nailed to the pillory, branded and sentenced to hard labour for life. Not surprisingly, as the Puritans gained strength, Laud's position became increasingly precarious.

Charles I was finally forced by money shortages to recall Parliament in 1640, after a break of eleven years. One of its first acts was to impeach Archbishop Laud for treason and send him to the Tower. He languished there for years until his trial and eventual execution on Tower Hill.

DOCTOR RICHARD VALPY, HEADMASTER OF READING SCHOOL, 1754–1836

Dr Valpy, who gave his name to Valpy Street, was probably Reading's greatest teacher. He rescued Reading School from closure and turned it into a flourishing place of learning. Born in

Doctor Valpy.

Jersey, he was educated in Normandy, Southampton, Guildford and Pembroke College, Oxford. In 1781, at the age of just twenty-seven, he was appointed the headmaster of Reading School. It was a post he was to hold for the next forty-nine years.

The post initially looked a most unpromising one. The school had few pupils, little money and decrepit buildings. Valpy had to undertake a good deal of new building at his own expense. It was a risky business. If the school still did not succeed, he stood to lose his entire investment. None the less, he went ahead with an ambitious building programme. A new school room, on the site of what is now the museum and art gallery on Valpy Street, was completed in 1786. By 1790, he had also provided a boarding house and an extension to the master's house.

He was awarded his doctorate in divinity in 1792 and was known thereafter as 'The Doctor'. The pupils had their own names for him, including 'Doctor Wackerback' and 'The Mighty Flogger', for Valpy was renowned as one of the most unyielding disciplinarians of the day. One of his favourite forms of correction was a 'smoul', a backhander around the face. Before going into his room for punishment, pupils would sit on a nearby stone, reputed to be particularly cold, in an effort to numb their behinds. Despite this, he seems to have enjoyed the respect and even affection of his pupils. He was said to have been a charming man, although the writer Mary Mitford (see p. 171) thought he was as vain as a peacock. He showed a great sense of humour in dealing with the pupils.

His teaching methods were often unconventional. He gave the boys financial rewards for doing well in exams. Good deeds by the pupils were rewarded by partial or full exemption from future punishment. They learned to swim – a cause which Valpy passionately supported – by him throwing half-crowns into the river, wrapped in white paper. Valpy was also a lavish entertainer. He used to buy the entire school a feast at an inn in Sonning each year and was a notorious gambler, helping to relieve Dr Mitford (father of Mary Mitford) of much of his fortune.

Like many a teacher, Valpy was an aspiring actor who loved school plays. The school's productions, for which he personally supervised every detail, were awaited eagerly by the local population. One of their productions of Shakespeare was even performed at Covent Garden. Valpy was not above 'improving'

Shakespeare, cutting parts out and adding speeches of his own (usually of a patriotic nature, with unpleasant references to the French). On one occasion, all attempts at rehearsal to get a pupil to act out a convincing display of fear and subservience were unsuccessful. Valpy solved the problem on the first night by giving the child a terrific clout immediately before he went on stage. The child's performance that night was highly praised! One of the purposes of his dramatic productions was to raise money for charities – a single production raised £130, an impressive sum for those days. Valpy was always anxious that the pupils should understand the needs of those less fortunate than themselves. He particularly supported the work of the Royal Humane Society and was also in the habit of adopting unfortunates. These included a one-legged boot black called Billy Boots and an elderly crone whose theatrical career had gone into decline due to the effects of gin.

Valpy ran the school until well into his seventies, before handing over the care of the school in 1830 to his son, Frank. Even then, he continued to take classes, but his eyesight was failing rapidly. Friends, including Miss Mitford and former prime minister Lord Sidmouth, continued to visit him. By 1832, he was completely blind and his beloved library of books was auctioned off. Valpy died in 1836 in Kensington and was buried at Kensal Green Cemetery.

Under Valpy, Reading School gained a national reputation. The school was recommended to the artist Gainsborough, who considered sending his children there, and several of Valpy's pupils went on to become distinguished figures in the law, academic life and the church. (Valpy himself was ordained as a vicar at the age of twenty-three and twice refused a bishopric.) By the time of his retirement, numbers at the school were up to two hundred, drawn from all over the world. It subsequently fell into a decline, from which it did not recover until its relocation to London Road in 1871.

HENRY ADDINGTON, FIRST VISCOUNT SIDMOUTH,
PRIME MINISTER, 1757–1844

Henry Addington's father, Anthony, was a medical man of some prominence, and his career was to shape the course of his son's life in an unexpected way. Originally from Twyford, Anthony settled in Reading in 1744, marrying the daughter of the headmaster of Reading School. He left Reading for London in 1754, so Henry was not a native of the town.

Among the patients Anthony Addington treated were the family of Lord Chatham. He restored the health of Chatham's second son, William Pitt, and a lifelong friendship developed between him and Henry Addington. On his retirement, Anthony Addington returned to Reading, where he gave free treatment to the poor of the town. He was called out of retirement to treat 'mad' King George III, which he did with some success. The family home, at 73 London Street, still stands.

Henry Addington studied at Winchester and Brasenose College, Oxford. When he graduated in 1778 he planned a career in the law, but it was William Pitt who persuaded him to pursue a political career instead. He was elected MP for Devizes in 1783. Towards the end of that year, Pitt formed his first administration, with Henry Addington one of his staunchest supportors. Although he hardly ever spoke in Parliament, Addington was liked by many of his colleagues and Pitt used his influence in 1789 to secure for him the post of Speaker. He held this post, with some success, for the next eleven years.

During his time as Speaker, Addington owned Woodley Lodge (later called Bulmershe Court), which stood on the site of Bulmershe Manor. He used it as a summer residence and was active in setting up a volunteer force, the Woodley Cavalry, to help counter the threat from Napoleon. Consisting of three officers and fifty-four men (with Addington himself in command), the Woodley Cavalry had their barracks in a row of old cottages in Church Road Earley. The nearby Three Tunns Inn was used to plan many of their activities. Many of the leading families of the county were represented in the cavalry. George III, Pitt and most of the royal family inspected the troops in 1799 and were entertained at Woodley Lodge.

Addington was a staunch anti-Catholic and a hard-line Unionist. When Pitt resigned and Addington was asked to form a government, many of the ablest politicians of the day refused to serve under him. He formed a second-rate government and many saw him as a mere caretaker until Pitt's return. As the *Dictionary of National Biography* put it: 'His industry and good intentions could not make up for his own dullness and the incapacity of his colleagues. The pompous manner and sententious gravity which became the Speaker's chair was ill-suited for debate.' Indeed, the only event of note during his premiership was the Treaty of Amiens in 1802, which brought a temporary lull to the war with France. The treaty was initially popular in the country, but Addington was too ready to trust Napoleon. He failed to prepare for renewed fighting as the danger signals grew clearer. By 1803, war was renewed and opposition to Addington's ministry was mounting. He was forced to resign in 1804 and was made Viscount Sidmouth in the following year. He continued to serve in the governments of the day as lord president of the council.

Sidmouth remained a zealous and intolerant churchman and in 1811 he introduced a Bill which would have required all dissenting ministers to be registered. This caused an uproar which led to the Bill being thrown out by the House of Lords. In 1812, Sidmouth was made home secretary. It was a time of deep depression in the country. Work and food were both in short supply and the people's desperation led to riots. Sidmouth suppressed these with great severity. Fourteen Luddites were hanged in a single day in York. As the riots grew worse, Sidmouth sought more draconian powers to put them down. He called for the suspension of *habeas corpus* and the reintroduction of old laws forbidding seditious meetings. He also called for the local law enforcement authorities to take tougher action against dissenters. One group of magistrates took his advice, with tragic consequences.

One day in 1819, a crowd numbering an estimated sixty thousand gathered peacefully in St Peter's Fields, Manchester, to hear a speech by orator Henry Hunt. The magistrates called in the cavalry, who charged the crowd. In the panic, eleven people were killed. This became known as the Peterloo Massacre, and it was widely condemned throughout the country. Sidmouth's reaction was to send his thanks to the magistrates and the troops.

Sidmouth's parliamentary career continued until 1832, and he remained intolerant and reactionary to the end. His last speech in Parliament was to oppose Catholic emancipation and the last vote he took part in was to oppose the 1832 Reform Bill.

Sidmouth is remembered in Reading for the streets which bear his names and for his part in the construction of the Royal Berkshire Hospital. Ironically, the leading promoter of the hospital, Richard Oliver, was a Catholic.

WILLIAM HAVELL, ARTIST, 1782–1857

William Havell was possibly the nearest thing to a great painter that Reading has produced. Flaws in his character and changing fashions in art contributed to his failure to achieve the recognition he felt he deserved. As one art historian put it, he had 'the egoism of genius without being quite gifted with the ability'.

His family were said to have come over with William the Conqueror and owned property near Moulsford, until a 'spendthrift hunter' squandered the family inheritance and fled to America. William's father Luke was apprenticed to a Reading painter and glazier called Aycliffe Cole. While Cole was busy drinking himself to death, Luke learned the trade and became an art teacher. He taught at Reading School, where William – one of fourteen children – was a pupil under the redoubtable Dr Valpy.

On discovering William's talent, his father introduced him to a London engraver who taught him many of the techniques of artists like J.M.W. Turner and Thomas Girton. Recognition came early, in 1804, when William had three works exhibited at the

William Havell, a self-portrait.

Royal Academy, and he was invited to become a founder-member of what was to become the Watercolour Society. In 1807 his painting of Reading Abbey showed him to be similar to Turner in both composition and technique.

Havell's outspoken support for Turner and his natural arrogance did not make him universally popular. As Wordworth's patron, Sir George Beaumont, put it: he is 'an ingenious young man . . . if you can inspire him with a little humility, you will be of great service to him and facilitate his progress'.

Watercolours suffered a fall in popularity after 1810. This and the economic depression of the time made it much harder for artists to earn a living. Havell in 1815 challenged the British Institution to justify their earlier rejection of a painting (*Walnut Gathering at Petersham*) which he considered to be at least equal to the work of Turner. This rejection and the downturn in the market for his works led him to accept the post of artist with Lord Amherst's embassy to China in 1816. After they were received – none too warmly – by the Chinese royal family, Havell found his way to India, where he managed to make money painting portraits and landscapes. An attack of cholera laid him low and he returned to England in poor health in 1826.

He found England no more prosperous than when he had left it and his style of painting was increasingly unfashionable. He decided to join the colony of British artists – including Turner – who were in Italy at the time. There he stayed with fellow artist Thomas Unwins, who admired Havell's work enormously but again found his overbearing manner hard to take. The climate and the food also disagreed with Havell and he returned home fairly quickly. The admiration he had found for his work in Italy was not repeated at home. Although he exhibited steadily until the end of his life, few of his works sold in London. Such sales as he made were for modest sums in provincial exhibitions.

He returned to some kind of prominence in 1839 when he became involved in the earliest days of photography. In that year, Havell demonstrated examples of 'photogenic drawing' at the Royal Academy. But Havell fell out with Fox Talbot, who suspected him of trying to steal his invention. The death of Havell's brother and collaborator, Frederick, finally ended any further experiments in this field.

The collapse of a bank in India led to Havell's financial ruin. He was reduced to scratching around for small commissions for portraits in order to make a living. Even so, some of his work in the 1850s still shows the spark of his earlier gifts. Then, during a visit to Reading late in 1857, his health began to deteriorate at dramatic speed. He returned home to Kensington, where he died on 16 December 1857.

For all his undoubted talent, William Havell's work is little known today. Had he remained part of the artistic mainstream, his reputation would surely have been greater. But his arrogance made it difficult for him to work either with the Academy or with patrons.

MARY RUSSELL MITFORD, WRITER, 1787–1855

Mary Russell Mitford was born in Alresford in Hampshire, the daughter of a doctor and the granddaughter of a wealthy clergyman. The family claimed descent from Sir Robert Bertram, who came to England with William the Conqueror. Both parents were well off when she was born and at the age of ten their fortunes were improved yet further when she won £20,000 in a lottery. Unfortunately her father was a hopeless gambler and spendthrift. She was to spend much of her life writing in an effort to support herself and her parents. Despite this, she appears to have been a devoted and loving daughter. Flushed with his new-found wealth, her father brought them to live in Reading at 39 London Road, a house which survives to this day. Mary herself was sent off to a boarding school in Chelsea.

In the early years of the nineteenth century, Dr Mitford bought land at Grazeley, where he demolished an Elizabethan house and built a new family home – Bertram House. But by 1820, he had squandered the entire family fortune. They left Bertram House penniless and came to live in Three Mile Cross.

Mary Mitford's literary career started with poetry and drama, in which she enjoyed only modest success. It was when she started to write fiction that she found her true medium and her great success began. Her real gift was for charming studies of country manners, scenery and character. When her accounts of 'Our Village' were serialised in the *Lady's Magazine*, its circulation rocketed. These were later collected into five volumes between the years 1824 and 1832. She soon became one of the most celebrated literary figures of the day. Charles Lamb and others sang her praises and her readers made regular pilgrimages to see Three Mile Cross, the village on which her stories were based. She became a close friend of Elizabeth Barrett Browning.

Although by all accounts a charming friend and companion, Mary Mitford was by no means a beauty. Short and stout, and with a bad complexion, she none the less had the most beautiful eyes. Charles Kingsley described them thus: 'Gleaming under a great deep globular brow, two such eyes as I never, perhaps, saw in any other Englishwoman . . . the glitter and depth, too, of eyes like coals'. The portrait of her in her autobiography *Notes of a Literary Life* (1852), fails to do justice to them, though it is said to improve upon nature in other respects.

She was never particularly fond of Reading and Reading people, which formed the basis for her novel *Belford Regis*. Although she had some close friends in the town – among them Thomas Noon Talfourd, the Liberal MP – she cared much less for some of the others she came into contact with, including Dr Valpy.

Her financial position was eased somewhat in later life by a Civil List pension of £100 a year, granted to her by Queen Victoria in 1839. After her father's death, some five years later, a public subscription was raised to pay off his debts.

Mary Mitford wrote right up to the end of her life. Her novel *Atherton* was only completed the year before her death. She was in poor health in her final years and died shortly after a carriage accident. She is buried in Swallowfield, to where she had moved in 1851.

AMELIA 'ANNIE' DYER, MURDERESS, 1839–96

Annie Dyer was hanged at Newgate on 10 June 1896. She had spent only the last of her fifty-seven years in Reading, but in that time she had become Reading's most celebrated murderess, a figure so reviled that she earned a place in Madame Tussaud's Chamber of Horrors.

She was born and spent most of her life in Bristol. Although from a respectable family, she married a mysterious and allegedly violent character called William Dyer, from whom she was later separated. In 1880, she served a short term of imprisonment for running an illegal baby farm. In November 1891 she made a suicide attempt that led to her spending some time in Gloucester Asylum. This was the first of several suicide attempts, but it is thought that they may have been staged, to try

Annie Dyer, from a contemporary newspaper photograph.

and throw investigators off the scent of earlier crimes. In September 1895, Annie Dyer moved to Elm Road in Lower Caversham, staying with members of her family. Very soon after, she moved to Piggotts Road, Caversham, where she started taking in children.

In Victorian times, there was great shame attached to having an illegitimate child. There was a ready market for people who would take in these children for a cash lump sum and regular payments towards their upkeep. Through advertisements in the paper and contacts in the west country, Dyer was soon able to take a large number of children into her care. She conducted her business under the alias Mrs Thomas, allegedly to conceal her whereabouts from her violent ex-husband. Then the corpse of a baby girl was found floating in the Thames by a bargeman on 30 March 1896. It had been strangled with tape. It was wrapped in brown paper and – an amazing piece of incompetence on the part of Dyer – it bore the name and address of Mrs Thomas, Piggotts Road, Caversham. Unfortunately, Dyer had by now moved again, to 45 Kensington Road. The delay in tracking her to her new address cost the lives of at least two more of her charges.

A few days later, a carpet bag was found in the Thames. It contained the bodies of four-month-old Doris, the daughter of unmarried mother Eleanor Marman of Cheltenham, and thirteen-month-old Henry, son of a lady's maid from London. Dyer was arrested on 4 April. While she was being questioned, the true scale of her crime began to become clearer. By the end of April, a total of seven infants had been recovered from the Thames. Dyer eventually provided a written confession to murder, largely in an attempt to prevent her daughter Mary being tried as an accessory to the crimes. On 2 May 1896, she was committed for trial. Two further suicide attempts were made while she was being held in custody.

The trial took place on 21 and 22 May. Counsel for the defence entered a plea of guilty but insane. Doctors were called from the mental asylums in which she had been a patient to vouch for her insanity. The prosecution in turn called evidence to show that her madness was feigned. Her daughter was found not guilty as an accessory to murder, but Annie Dyer received the death sentence.

We will never know how many children she murdered. The number was at least seven and probably eleven, and one estimate puts the number as high as fifty, during her long career as a 'child minder'.

RUFUS ISAACS, FIRST MARQUIS OF READING, 1860–1935

A statue in the gardens at Eldon Square commemorates one of the most remarkable men ever to serve as MP for Reading. In his lifetime he was attorney general, lord chief justice, ambassador to the United States of America, viceroy of India and foreign secretary. He had a string of titles and honours and was the first commoner to rise to the title of marquess since the Duke of Wellington. He achieved all this despite being hammered on the stock market in the depression of 1884, despite being involved in the Marconi scandal of 1912 and, most of all, despite being Jewish. Emancipation for the Jews only began in 1830 and it was around the time of his birth that they got full political rights, including the right to sit in Parliament. The first Jewish QC was not appointed until in 1858 (Francis Goldsmid, whose Reading connections are remembered in the name of Goldsmid Road) and the appointment of the first Jewish judge did not follow until in 1873. Lord Rothschild became the first Jewish peer in 1886.

Rufus Isaacs.

Isaacs was born the son of fruit importer and shipbroker in Spitalfields, London. After a cosmopolitan education that took him to Brussels and Hanover, it was intended that he should go to Cambridge University before joining the family business. Instead, he ran away to sea on board a collier bound for Rio. He soon learned that the sea was not for him and tried to desert in Rio. He failed and had to sail all round the world to get home. On his return he spent three years in the family business and eight as a stockbroker's clerk. Although he demonstrated a prodigious memory for facts and figures, the fact that he accumulated losses of £8,000 showed him that the business world was not for him. During his last three years of stockbroking, he studied for the Bar and began practising as a barrister in 1887.

His abilities soon became known. He broke away from the traditional bullying style of cross-examination favoured by leading counsel such as Sir Charles Russell. His style was instead urbane and polite – 'deadly fair play' as one rival counsel put it. He soon came to be involved in the leading cases of the day – prosecuting a libel case for the brother of Joseph Chamberlain and securing a conviction in the Desson Hall Murder case. His skills and his prodigious capacity for hard work – his working day started at 5 a.m. and went on until late at night – meant that he became a king's counsel within eleven years. Later, as a judge, he was responsible for passing the death sentence on the Irish patriot Sir Roger Casement.

In 1904, the sitting MP for Reading, George William Palmer, decided to stand down due to ill-health. He was a Liberal and Isaac's liberal reputation encouraged the local party to choose him as Palmer's successor. Much was against him. The seat was a marginal one and his rival was a man with local links and the support of major businesses, such as Suttons and Simonds. But Isaacs campaigned (under the slogan 'Rufus for Reading') for universal comprehensive education and trade union rights. His devastating courtroom skills were used to good effect on the hustings. With the help of guest speakers, including Lloyd George and Winston Churchill (at that time a Liberal), he won the seat.

Isaacs looked around for a home in the Reading area and settled on Foxhill, just outside the borough on the Whiteknights estate. He lived there for twelve years, entertaining the leading lights of the political and artistic world. He finally sold the property to Lord Hirst, founder of the General Electric Company, in 1917. Isaacs remained MP for Reading until 1913, when his appointment as lord chief justice forced him to give up the seat. It also brought him a title, and he chose to be Lord Reading of Erleigh. He was also made a freeman of the borough.

During the First World War, Isaacs was made ambassador to the United States, where he was largely responsible for raising the first allied war loan and getting President Wilson to dispatch troops to France. Between 1921 and 1926 he was viceroy of India, confronted by the resistance of Gandhi and his followers. On his return, he was made Marquis of Reading and his career in public life ended as foreign secretary to the National Government in 1931.

The statue to him in Eldon Square originally stood in the Central Place of New Delhi. After independence they no longer wanted this reminder of their colonial past. Isaac's widow paid for it to be returned to England and the council erected it in the gardens of Eldon Square in 1971.

History in a Name

As the earlier sections of this book show, the names of streets and places in Reading are often a permanent reminder of some part of their history. Here are some examples:

Addington Road Henry Addington was the son of a Reading doctor who succeeded William Pitt as prime minister. He was later rewarded by being made Lord Sidmouth and Sidmouth Street is also named after him.

Arthur Hill Baths Arthur Hill was a Reading-based manufacturer of rubber goods who was elected to the council in 1876.

Battle, Battle Hospital, Battle School William the Conqueror founded an abbey near Hastings to celebrate his victory in the battle there. Among the lands he gave to it was an estate to the north-west of Reading, formerly owned by St Mary's church. The abbey was called Battle and the name survives in this area of Reading to this day.

Beansheaf Farm From the fourteenth century family who owned the land. John Beansheaf granted land in Tilehurst to John Stonor in 1316.

Blagrave Street John Blagrave was a mathematician who lived at Southcote Manor. The family had extensive land holdings in Reading and he was a benefactor to the town in a number of ways. There is a monument to him in St Laurence's church. One member of the family, Daniel Blagrave, was MP for Reading and a signatory to the death warrant of King Charles I.

Brigham Road Anthony Brigham was cofferer to King Henry VIII. He bought the empty shell of the chapel of Our Lady in Caversham at the time of the dissolution of the monasteries.

Buckside A small street by the river in Caversham. Eels were caught there in large traps called bucks.

Cadogan Place Named after the Earl of Cadogan, lord high steward of Berkshire, during the eighteenth century.

Castle Street, Castle Hill Reading once had a castle, but nobody now knows where it was. It was thought to have been built by

177

King Stephen and destroyed by Henry II. It would seem reasonable to assume that it was somewhere at the top of the Castle Hill.

Caversham   There are a variety of explanations of this name and no less than twenty-two different spellings! These include 'Caves Sha' – a wooded hollow, the home of somebody called Cavers and the home of calves.

Chain Street   During the seventeenth century a chain was erected across Minster Street at this point to control access to it. In the sixteenth century it was known as Grope Lane.

Coldicutt Street, Caversham   William Coldicutt was a Caversham butcher who kept cattle in a field off Gosbrook Road. He sold the land in 1842, but the street built there kept his name.

Craven Road   William, Lord Craven, acquired Caversham Park before the Civil War. He lost it at the end of the war but it was restored to him by King Charles II. William Craven was alleged to have been the lover of Charles I's sister.

Crawshay Drive   The Crawshay family were ironmasters, one of whose number founded the iron works at Merythr Tydfil. They lived in Caversham Park from the 1820s to 1922.

De Montfort Island (later known as Fry's Island)   This island in the middle of the Thames was chosen as the site for a duel between Robert de Montfort and Henry of Essex in the year 1163. De Montfort accused Essex of treason and cowardice during a battle. Henry II witnessed the duel, in which Essex was almost mortally wounded. The monks of Reading Abbey took him back to the Abbey, where he recovered and spent the rest of his life living in retreat.

Downshire Square   The Marquis of Downshire was the lord high steward of Berkshire in around 1865.

Emmer Green   Thought to derive from the Saxon 'Eamere' – a lake beside a stream.

Forbury   From 'Fore-berrie'. A berrie is a wide open space, making this a wide open space in front of the town. Another possibility is that it comes from Faubourg, or suburb, meaning an area which lay beyond the jurisdiction of the borough magistrates.

Garrard Street   Named after William Garrard, who has been described as 'an influential resident'.

Goldsmid Road   Francis Goldsmid was a lawyer and member of parliament for Reading. The family owned the Whiteknights estate until it was bought by Reading University in 1947.

Gosbrook Road   Formerly Goose Brook Lane. A stream used to flow across the water meadows here into the Thames.

Great Knollys Street The Knollys family were major land-owners in the area, including the land on which Great Knollys Street was built in the nineteenth century. During the sixteenth century Sir Francis Knollys (then spelt Knolles) was the owner of Caversham Park. His wife Catherine was first cousin to Queen Elizabeth I.

Jesse Terrace Thomas Jesse acquired the land on which it stands in 1802.

Katesgrove From Cattle Grove or Kattel's Grove.

Kentwood Hill Nicholas Kentwood is listed as one of the parishioners in this area in 1341.

King's Road and Queen's Road These were built in 1832 on former Crown land and were named after King William IV and Queen Adelaide.

King Street Built in 1760 by Alderman John Richards, a local draper. It was named to mark the coronation of King George III.

Liebenrood Road John Engelbert Liebenrood bought the Mansion House in nearby Prospect Park in about 1800 and greatly extended it.

McIlroy Park William McIlroy was the founder of McIlroy's department store, which stood on Oxford Road opposite what is now Broad Street Mall.

Marsack Street The Marsack family bought Caversham Park in the early 1780s. Major Charles Marsack had recently retired from the East India Company and was alleged to be an illegitimate son of George II by the Comtesse de Marsac, a Huguenot who came over with the Hanoverian court.

Orts Road In the days when the Abbey flourished, the poor people of Reading used to assemble outside the south-eastern gate of the Abbey to collect the orts, or leftover scraps of food from the monks' tables.

Pincent's Farm Edmund Pincent acquired land from the Abbot of Reading in 1316.

Portman Road Named after the Portman Brook, which used to flow nearby.

Rabson's Recreation Ground John Rabson was the chairman of the borough council's public health committee around the time of the boundary extension to take in Caversham in 1911. He was first elected to the council in 1906 and was one of its first Labour members.

Reading Various suggestions have been made about its derivation. 'Red' or 'Rea' means an overflowing and 'ing' a

179

meadow. This could refer to the floodplain of the Kennet in the Seven Bridges area. Another suggestion is Rhyd Hen (Old Ford) or Read-ing (the property of Reada – the Red – whose followers were called Readingas).

Routh Lane   Martin Joseph Routh was rector of Tilehurst for forty-four years and president of Magdalen College, Oxford for sixty-three years. He died in 1854, aged ninety-nine. His nephew succeeded him as rector of Tilehurst from 1855–1905, creating a remarkable family 'dynasty' of almost one hundred years as rector.

Sidmouth Street   See Addington Road.

Silver Street   This was formerly called Sievier Street, and sieve-making was carried out there.

Stanshawe Road   Robert Stanshawe was a groom of the king's chamber in the reign of Henry VIII. He bought the land on which Stanshawe Road now stands when Greyfriars church was dissolved.

Talfourd Avenue   Thomas Noon Talfourd was born in Reading in 1795, the son of a local brewer. He became a lawyer, MP for Reading, a judge, a friend of Charles Dickens (who himself was once invited to stand as MP for Reading) and the father of the Copyright Act of 1842, which did much to protect authors from piracy.

Thorn Walk   This was Thorn Street until it disappeared under the Inner Distribution Road. Possibly named after George Thorn, three times mayor of Reading between 1636 and 1663, and a fanatical persecutor of Quakers.

Tilehurst   The most obvious explanation is that it relates to the tile and brick-making industry that flourished there. An alternative may be that in the fourteenth century it was known as 'Tyghel hurst', a 'wooded height' or a 'house or station in a wood'.

Vachel Road   The Vachells were a major landowning family in Reading. Thomas Vachell was MP for Reading at the time of the dissolution of Reading Abbey and bought the land on which Vachel Road stands.

Valpy Street   Dr Richard Valpy became master of Reading School in 1781 and held the post for forty-nine years.

Vanlore Way   Sir Peter Vanlore was a rich cloth merchant from Utrecht, who came to live in Tilehurst in 1604. He built a house at Calcot Park in about 1620, on the site of the present Calcot Park House.

The Warren   Sir Richard Blount of Mapledurham House built a road beneath Chauzes Wood in around 1600, linking his house to Caversham. The name refers to the estate's rabbit warren. Many large estates had these, which were carefully farmed for their meat.

Watlington Street   Robert Watlington was a wealthy cloth maker in Reading. One of his sons, Samuel, built Watlington House in 1688 and was mayor of Reading on four occasions.

Yield Hall Lane   This was the original location for the town's yield hall or guild hall.

Zinzan Street   The Zinzans were a Reading landowning family of Italian extraction. They lived at Calcot Park in the seventeenth century.

A List of Sources

Alexander, Alan, *Borough Government and Politics: Reading 1835–1985*. George Allen and Unwin, 1985.

Arnold, H.J.B., *William Henry Fox Talbot – Pioneer of Photography and Man of Science*. Hutchinson Benham, 1977.

Asser, Michael, *The Royal County*. Berkshire County Council, 1977.

Babbage, Terry, *Tylehurst Described – An Historical Account*. Berkshire County Council.

Baines, John, *The Life of William Laud*. Joseph Masters, 1855.

Beckett, Derrick, *Brunel's Britain*. David and Charles.

Berkshire Federation of Women's Institutes, *The Old Berkshire Village Book*. Countryside Books, 1979.

Childs, W.M., *Reading During the Early Part of the 19th Century*. Reading University College, 1910.

——, *Notes on the Town of Reading in the 17th Century*. Reading University College Review, December 1914.

Cooper, J.J., *Some Worthies of Reading*. The Swarthmore Press, 1923.

Darter, W.S., *Reminiscences of Reading by an Octogenarian*. 1888.

Department of the Environment, *List of Buildings of Special Architectural or Historic Interest – Borough of Reading*. HMSO, 1947 and subsequent amendments.

Dictionary of National Biography. Smith, Elder, 1885.

Dobson, Elizabeth A, 'The Conservation of Patterned Brick Terraces in Reading'. M. Phil. Dissertation, University of Reading, 1985.

Doran, J. *The History of Reading*. Charles Ingall, 1835.

Dowsett, G.R., *The Municipal and Parish Church of St Laurence in Reading*. British Publishing Company.

Fines, John, *Dr Richard Valpy – Headmaster of Reading School*. 1967.

Gibbon, Perceval, *Rufus Isaacs, A Great Jew*. McClures, 1914.
Godwin Arnold, H., *Town Trail 1*. Reading Civic Society.
Good, V.R., *The Most Ancient Church of Reading*.

Handbooks for Reading of 1882, 1892, 1906 and 1949.
Harrison, W., *Reading and Some of its Literary Associations*. Book Auction Records, 1911.
Historic Notes on the Parish Church of St Mary the Virgin. 1914.
Humphreys, A.L., *The Streets and Street Lore of Reading*. Published privately, 1926.
Hyde, H., *Montgomery – Lord Reading*. Heinemann, 1967.

Jones, John B., *Sketches of Reading*. Lovejoy, 1870.

Kift, Mary, *Life in Old Caversham*. Published privately, 1980.
Kinder, R.W., *The Reading to Tonbridge Line*. The Oakwood Press, 1974.

MacDermot, E.T., *The History of the Great Western Railway, volume 1*. Ian Allen, 1964.
Man, J., *The Stranger in Reading*. Snare and Man, 1810.
Marshall, J.G.B., *Report on the Sewerage of Reading*. Local Board of Health, 1858.
Milwards, *The Milward Story*. 1957.
Minchell, Ruth and Jonathon, *Bridges over the Thames*. Blandford Press, 1985.

Naxton, Michael, *The History of Reading School*. Reading School, 1986.
North, Leslie, *Royal Reading's Colourful Past*. Cressrelles, 1979.

Owen, Felicity, *The Life and Work of William Havell*. Bicentenary Exhibition Catalogue, 1981.

Phillips, Daphne, *The Story of Reading*. Countryside Books, 1980.
——, *How the Great Western came to Berkshire*. Berkshire Books.

Railton, M. and Barr, M., *The Royal Berkshire Hospital 1839–1989*.
Read, John, *Reading Seventy Years Ago*. 1887.

Reading Borough Council, *Reading, Our Architectural Heritage.* 1975.

Reading Libraries, *Inns of Reading.* Berkshire County Council, 1974.

Reading Museum and Art Gallery, *Reading Walkabout Guide.*

Reading University, Extra Mural Department, *Reading 1540–1640: A Portrait of a Community.* 1980.

Reading Yearbook. Turner Bros. 1880.

Redlands Local History Group, *Old Redlands.* 1990.

Searing, Roger, *Down Memory Lane: Reading between the Wars.* Reading Chronicle/Countryside Books, 1985.

Searle, Muriel V., *Down the Line to Bristol.* Baton Transport, 1986.

Sherwood, K.M., *The Story of Tilehurst and its Parish Church.*

Snow, V.F. and Thomas D.B., *The Talbotype Establishment in Reading 1844–7. The Photographic Journal,* February 1966.

Southerton, P.G., *The Story of a Prison.* Osprey, 1975.

——, *Reading in Old Photographs.* Alan Sutton, 1988.

Trevor-Roper, Hugh, *Archbishop Laud.* Macmillan, 1962.

Vaughan, A., *A Pictorial Record of Great Western Architecture.* Oxford Publishing Co., 1977.

Waters, Laurence, *Rail Centres – Reading.* Ian Allen, 1990.

Whitehouse, P. and St John Thomas, D., *The Great Western Railway: 150 Glorious Years.* David and Charles, 1984.

Wilson, Patrick, *Murderess.* Michael Joseph, 1971.

Index